FileMaker Pro 2.1 *for Macintosh*

FileMaker Pro 2.1
for Macintosh

by Adam Greif

FileMaker Pro 2.1 for Macintosh
Visual QuickStart Guide

Copyright © 1994 by Adam Greif/Computer Generation Ltd.

Peachpit Press, Inc.
2414 Sixth Street
Berkeley, CA 94710

Cover Design: Studio Silicon

Distribution

Peachpit Press books are distributed to the U.S. book trade by Publishers Group West, 4065 Hollis, P.O. Box 8843, Emeryville, CA 94609, phone: 800/788-3123 or 510/658-3453, fax: 510/658-1834. Peachpit books are also available from wholesalers throughout the U.S. including Baker & Taylor Books, Golden-Lee Book Distributors, and Ingram Book Company. Resellers outside the book trade can contact Peachpit directly at 800/980-8999.

Notice of Rights

Notice of Liability

Author

Adam Greif is a journalist living in Paris, France, who has written several books about the Macintosh in French and English. He can be reached at the AppleLink address: Greif.

Thanks

To Kristin Barendsen for her very careful reading of this book.

ISBN: 1-56609-123-3

0 9 8 7 6 5 4 3 2 1

♺ Printed on Recycled Paper
Printed and bound in the United States of America

Contents

This book describes version 2.1 of FileMaker Pro for the Macintosh. Version 2.1 for Windows is quite similar.

There is only one small difference between version 2.0 and 2.1 for the Macintosh. See p. 7.

FileMaker Pro is a *Database* program. It allows you to store and organize data—text, numbers, pictures and QuickTime movies. Its powerful features then make it very easy to retrieve data, sort them, or change the way they are displayed and accessed.

This preliminary section presents subjects that you may need to look at before studying FileMaker Pro: Macintosh basics (files, folders, menus, keyboard); installing FileMaker Pro from its original floppy disks onto your Macintosh's hard disk; data storage—

PRELIMINARY

What you see on the screen when you turn on the Macintosh is called the *desktop*. Electronic *files* and *folders* are supposed to evoke the paper files and folders you shuffle on a wooden desk.

The first picture below shows the *catalog window* of a hard disk called "Macintosh HD." Here, the hard disk's files and folders are represented by *icons;* you can also display a catalog as a list of names. Icons exist for your convenience, but the computer needs names to locate files on the hard disk, floppy disk, CD-ROM, or whatever storage volume it can access.

ICONS
This window contains five folder icons, including one for a *Shared* folder which you can open from another network Macintosh.
The "Old Stuff" icon is highlighted (inverted), indicating that the Old Stuff folder is *selected* for action. You might open it, or duplicate it, or delete it.
"FileMaker Pro" is an *application program*, or an *application*.
"Addesses" is a *document* created with this application.

CLOSE BOX
Clicking this box closes the window.
This is similar to choosing the **Close** command in the **File** menu.

TITLE BAR
Dragging this bar moves the window around.

ZOOM BOX
Clicking this box makes the window big enough to show all its contents or fill the screen, or brings it back to its original size.

SCROLL BAR
In this example, some icons are hidden outside the window, and you might want to scroll them into sight.
Click the scroll bar *arrows* for a slow scroll, or drag the square *scroll box* for a fast one. Click above or under the scroll box to scroll by one full window length.

POINTER
The black arrow is the *pointer*. It is driven by the mouse.

SIZE BOX
Dragging this box lets you change the size of the window.

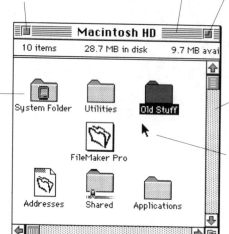

MOUSE
To *click* means "to press and release the mouse button."
To *drag* means "to move the mouse while its button is down."
When a key like Shift or Option is pressed at the same time, MacSpeak verbs are used: *Shift-click, Option-click, Shift-drag, Option-drag,* etc.

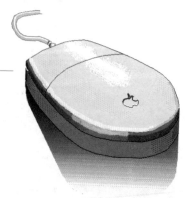

The *menu bar* above the desktop lets you pull down *menus* and choose *commands*. In this book, menu names and commands are written in **bold** letters.

COMMANDS

Commands like **Open** and **Print** are dimmed because they are not available. To make them available, you should tell the computer what file you want to open or print—i.e., you should select a file's icon.

⌘**N** is a "keyboard shortcut" for the **New Folder** command. The ⌘ symbol stands for the Command key. (See key names on the next page.)

You can create a new folder by holding down the Command key and pressing "N". Try it!

ELLIPSIS

When a command is followed by an ellipsis (i.e. three dots...), choosing it displays a dialog box where you enter additional info before launching the command.

Clickable areas in a dialog box, like *More Choices, Cancel* and *Find* below, are called buttons.

Pressing the Return or Enter key is a shortcut for clicking a button with a thick border, like *Find*.

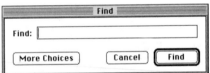

COPYING A FILE

When you drag an icon from one window to another, two different things can happen.

If both windows represent folders belonging to the same disk, the file is moved from the first folder to the second one.

If the windows do not belong to the same disk, as in the example at right (where *Blue Planet* is a folder on the 80MB hard disk and *Backup5* is an empty 800K floppy disk), the file is copied.

Actually, you can drag the file's icon to the floppy's icon—you do not need to open the floppy's window.

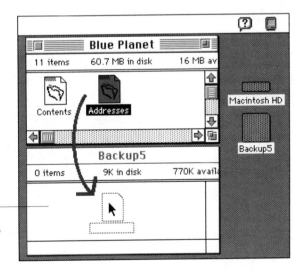

PRELIMINARY

As you'll notice, the Macintosh keyboard has some more keys than a typewriter keyboard. Their FileMaker Pro usage is explained below.

The keyboard below is that of a standard Macintosh LC. The location of some keys may be different on other models.

The *extended* keyboard, which usually comes with Quadras, features still more keys for shortcuts.

TAB
In Word Processing programs (e.g., Microsoft Word), pressing the Tab key sends the insertion point to the next tab stop.
In FileMaker Pro, it sends the insertion point to the next text field.
The Tab key also sends the insertion point to the next field inside dialog boxes.

BACKSPACE
This key is also called Delete. Pressing it deletes the last letter you typed, or a selected text or item.

RETURN
This key inserts a *hard return* or *paragraph character* into text.
In a dialog box, it is equivalent to the Enter key (see below).

OPERATORS
The /, *, -, + keys let you divide, multiply, subtract and add numbers.

CAPS-LOCK

SHIFT

CONTROL
Some programs —but not FileMaker Pro—use this key in keyboard shortcuts.

OPTION
This key lets you type special characters: see opposite page.
It is also used in keyboard shortcuts.

COMMAND
This key is often called the *Apple* key by ignoramuses, but it is officially the *Command* key.
Pressing it in combination with a letter lets you choose a command without pulling down a menu.
Such *shortcuts* are shown inside the menus as ⌘**A**, ⌘**O**, etc.

ESCAPE
This key selects the number on the Status Area *Book* (see p. 16).
In a dialog box, it is a shortcut for *Cancel*.

ARROWS
These keys let you move the insertion point in a text, or a selected item in Layout mode.

ENTER
This key lets you "validate" an entry inside a field.
In a dialog box, it is a shortcut for clicking a thick-bordered button marked, for example, *OK* or *Open*.

Keyboard

Special characters, accessed by pressing Option or Shift-Option in combination with letters, may vary slightly from one font to another. Note that you should avoid them if you ever want to read the files in a Windows environment.

Accents (shown inside parentheses) modify the next character you type.

OPTION

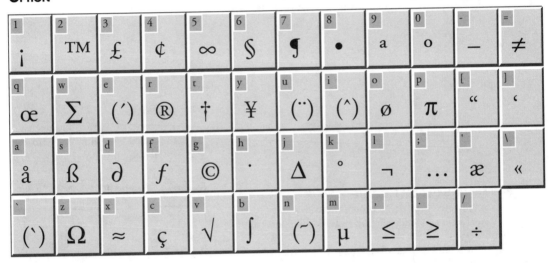

SHIFT-OPTION

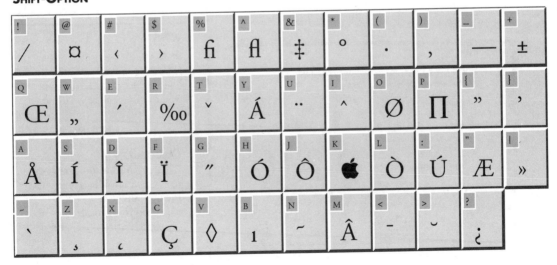

PRELIMINARY

If FileMaker Pro is already installed on your hard disk, you can skip these two pages.

Installing the program is quite easy. Insert the *Install 1* floppy disk into your disk drive and double-click the Installer icon.

Claris advises you to turn off any anti-virus program before you install the program. One way to do this is to restart your Macintosh while holding the Shift key down—until you see a panel saying "Welcome to Macintosh. Extensions off."

INSTALLER
Double-click this icon to display the dialog box below and start the installation process.

FILEMAKER BALLOON HELP.SIT
"sit" is short for "Stuff-It," a program that was used to *compact* the files. The installation process will "unstuff" them.

The compacted FileMaker Pro application is found on the *Install 2* disk.

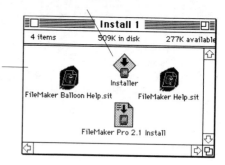

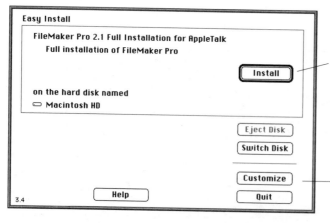

INSTALL
The program copies files from the first floppy disk, then asks you to insert the second one.

CUSTOMIZE
Clicking this button changes the dialog box into the one shown on the opposite page.

You need to customize in some "cross-platform" file-sharing situations.

Standard installation covers most situations: an independant Macintosh, a Macintosh belonging to a regular AppleTalk or EtherTalk network, and most cross-platform setups. Note that you can share files with FileMaker Pro for Windows and other programs.

You need custom MacIPX installation if the PC side uses Novell NetWare. This is the only new feature in version 2.1 of FileMaker Pro. See the *Installation Guide Addendum* (and your network administrator) to find out more about it.

COMPLETE OR CUSTOM

You need a little over 2MB of free space on your hard disk to install everything, or 600K if you install only the FileMaker Pro application.

The application, some *Templates* (models), examples, and a *Tutorial Folder* (which goes along with the "Getting Started" manual) are installed in a folder called *FileMaker Pro 2.1 Folder*.

Help (a must—see p. 53), dictionaries, and some other goodies are installed inside the System Folder in a folder called Claris.

```
Click the items you want to select;
Shift-click to select multiple items.

FileMaker Pro 2.1 Full Installation for AppleTalk
FileMaker Pro 2.1 Full Installation for MacIPX

FileMaker Pro 2.1 Application
FileMaker Network (AppleTalk Support)
FileMaker Network (MacIPX Support)
Macintosh Plus AppleTalk File

        FileMaker Network (MacIPX Support)
          Size:   174K
          Date:   Tue, Jun 15, 1993
          Version: 2.1
This option installs the FileMaker Network for MacIPX file and
the MacIPX Control Panel. These files are needed to network
FileMaker databases over the Novell network. The MacIPX
Control Panel has to be dragged to the System Folder.

                              Install

                           ⊂ Macintosh HD

                           Eject Disk
                           Switch Disk

                           Easy Install
                           Quit
```

PERSONALIZE

When you open FileMaker Pro for the very first time, this dialog box asks for your name. This is a symbolic protection against software piracy: you shouldn't install a program already labeled with somebody else's name. There is no barrier against such an installation, but it is forbidden by copyright law.

If the magazine used as an example in this book has twenty Macintosh computers and wants to use FileMaker Pro on all of them, it should buy twenty programs, or ask Claris for a special license.

Note that two copies of the same FileMaker Pro on a network won't open at the same time.

```
CLARIS®   Please personalize your copy of
          FileMaker Pro 2.1

          Name
          Greif
          Company

          Serial Number
          2639115

          Register your product now to receive our
          newsletter, updates, and upgrade notification.

          Cancel              OK
```

PRELIMINARY

The examples in this book feature a fictitious science magazine called *Blue Planet*—modelled after a real magazine.

Let's say your job consists in keeping track of all the articles published in *Blue Planet*. For years, you reigned over a strange kingdom of dark wooden file cabinets and deep drawers. The map to this kingdom was neatly folded inside your head!

When writers or editors needed some information, they came and had a nice chat with you while you opened drawers and sifted cards. Although you loved to explain your filing system to people, nobody ever understood it.

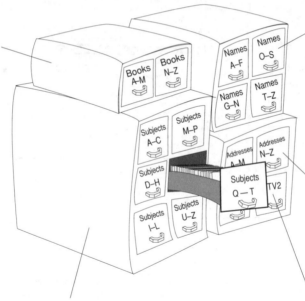

BOOKS
Books mentioned in *Blue Planet* articles were listed here in alphabetical order of titles.

NAMES
Cards for every *Blue Planet* contributor, listing his/her name and published articles, were kept here.
Cards were also created for most people mentioned in the articles.

ADDRESSES
Addresses were grouped by categories, such as journalists, science camps, universities, and so forth.

SUBJECTS
When an issue included an article about the pyramids, information about the article (its title, its author's name, and what issue of the magazine it was published in) was added to the *Antiquity*, *Archeology* and *Egypt* cards in the Subjects cabinet. This information was also entered on the author's card in the Names file cabinet.

TV
These drawers held information about the magazine's collection of videotapes.

Files

Blue Planet now uses Macintosh computers for desktop publishing and other tasks. The examples in this book will show how four simple FileMaker Pro files let you store and organize the information formerly kept in wooden file cabinets.

In the BASICS: USER section, you'll learn how to use a FileMaker Pro database that may have been designed by some computer wizard. Then you'll discover FileMaker Pro's *Browse* mode: it's like opening file drawers designed by a cabinet maker.

You'll study wizard tricks—cabinet making!—in the BASICS: DESIGNER section, which explores the program's *Layout* mode.

CONTENTS

This is the main file, which replaces the multiple *Subjects* files and the *Names* files. You now need to enter information about an article only once. FileMaker Pro lets you retrieve and sort data in ways that were impossible before. It also makes it much easier for other people to consult the files—bypassing the wonderful but fragile map hidden inside your head.

BOOKS

This file lets you retrieve a list of books written by a certain author, or published by a specific publisher. This was impossible with the wooden cabinets, where you could not find a book when you didn't know its title.

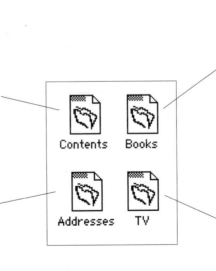

ADDRESSES

FileMaker Pro is great for professional address books. You can now find all the science camps in California, all the Montessori schools in America, etc.

TV

The names of the tapes are listed in alphabetical order, as in the old file cabinets, but now you can easily re-order tapes by subject, length, etc.

Records:

11

Unsorted

This section describes user features: browsing through the database, entering data, finding data, sorting records. In most Macintosh programs, you create and design documents for yourself: you decide that a title should be bold or a paragraph centered.

FileMaker Pro is different. Often, a person designs a database that will be used by other people. The designer can restrict the access of users to certain features. For example, users might be barred from the Layout mode altogether, so that they do not modify the basic design of the files.

Even if you plan to design a database—for yourself or for other people—you should study and understand user features first, since they represent the materials you'll put into shape with the tools described in the BASICS: DESIGNER section.

As the librarian of *Blue Planet*, you spend most of your time answering readers' and journalists' queries about past articles, but once a month you open the new issue of the magazine and, for every article, enter information into a basic FileMaker Pro unit called a "record." This builds the main file, which replaces the *Subjects* and *Names* cabinets. With the old system, an article was referenced in two or three *Subjects* files at most. Now, it is very easy to enter eight or nine subject keywords.

BOOK
This icon shows which record is active. Clicking a page lets you move to the next or previous record. See p. 18.

BOOKMARK
Dragging the *Bookmark* lets you browse through the database. See p. 18.

RECORD
A "record" lets you store information—here, the description of one *Blue Planet* article. A collection of records makes up a FileMaker Pro file, in this case called *Contents*.

HEADER
The *Header* is a part of the screen that remains constant as records change.

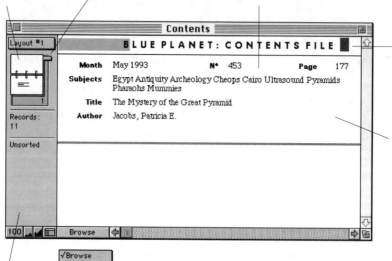

DATA
The information that you enter into the record is called "data."

STATUS AREA
The *Status Area* displays tools and information pertaining to the current mode.

MODE SELECTOR
There are four "modes" in FileMaker Pro: *Browse* (this page), *Find* (see p. 22), *Layout* (p. 32) and *Preview* (p. 73). The name of the current mode appears in a box at the bottom of the window—the *Mode Selector*. Clicking it displays a pop-up menu where you can choose another mode.

If you don't change the default settings, records are displayed one at a time, as on the opposite page. This type of display makes good sense for large unrelated records, like invoices.

Choosing **View as List** in the **Select** menu lets you display records as a scrolling list—see example below. On a large monitor, seven or eight records can be viewed at the same time.

HOW MANY

Eleven records make up this example file. A file can hold thousands of records.

It is said that a file with 50,000 records or so becomes sluggish. Before you build a big file, you should make sure that you have adequate backup hardware, such as a Syquest disk drive.

HEADER

The Header doesn't move when you scroll the list of records.

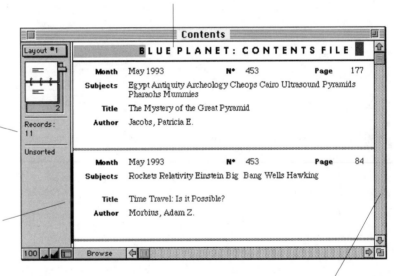

CURRENT RECORD

In a list, the current (or "active") record is marked by a black vertical bar on the left side.

Its number appears at the bottom right of the Book.

You can activate a record by clicking it or by using the Book.
See p. 16.

SCROLL

When records are *Viewed as List*, you can use the scroll bar as well as the Book to browse through the file.

While the Book displays a record *and makes it the active one*, the scroll bar only displays it.
See p. 17.

To begin entering data, you must first create a blank record by choosing **New Record** in the **Edit** menu, or by using the keyboard shortcut ⌘-**N**.

The new record appears at the very end of the file. In the example below, there are ten completed records; the new one is number 11. You might wish to create a new record between numbers 5 and 6, but you can't. If you know in advance that you'll eventually need a new record between numbers 5 and 6, put it there after you create number 5 and leave it empty until you need it. You can delete it at any time.

If you want to reorder a small file, you can also proceed in the following manner: Duplicate the record that you want to become #1, then the record you want to become #2, etc., by choosing the **Duplicate Record** command in the **Edit** menu. The duplicates appear at the end of the file. When all the records have been duplicated, delete the original records and keep the correctly ordered duplicates.

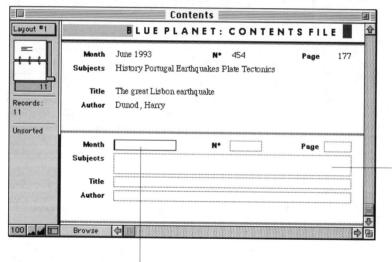

FIELD
Data goes into boxes called *fields*. When a record has just been created, or whenever you press the Tab key or click a field to write into it, all fields are made visible by dotted borders.

ACTIVE FIELD
A continuous border marks the active field—the field where the insertion point blinks.

To move the insertion point from one field to the next one, press the Tab key. To move it to the preceding one, press Shift-Tab.

The *Tab Order* feature lets you define which fields are "next" and "preceding." See p. 85.

You can't change the shape of a field in Browse mode, but you can enter more data into a field than its shape would seem to allow. The field will swell to include the full data as you enter it, but will shrink again as soon as you press the Tab or Enter key or close it in any other manner. Try it!

Month	May 1993	N°	453	Page	177
Subjects	Egypt Antiquity Archeology Cheops Cairo Ultrasound Pyramids Pharaohs Mummies				
Title	The Mystery of the Great Pyramid Reprinted from The Friends of the British Museum Quarterly				
Author					

HIDDEN DATA

When you're beginning to use FileMaker Pro, you may think that after entering the *Title* into the record above, you move to what appears to be the next line, i.e. *Author*, by pressing the Return key. This is wrong: you should press the Tab key, or click the mouse, to move to the *Author* field.

Pressing Return does something different: it adds a line to the field, enlarging it.

Typing a long text without pressing Return also enlarges the field; it will accommodate as many lines as necessary (up to 64,000 characters). The whole text is displayed only when the field is active. Otherwise, the field is truncated and any additional data is hidden (but is still considered by the Find feature).

Month	May 1993	N°	453	Page	177
Subjects	Egypt Antiquity Archeology Cheops Cairo Ultrasound Pyramids Pharaohs Mummies				
Title	The Mystery of the Great Pyramid*				
Author	Jacobs, Patricia E.				

A SIMPLE TRICK

You can mark a field that contains more data than meets the eye by typing some character, such as (*), before hitting Return.

Compare this picture to those on pp. 12 and 13, where no one would guess that the *Title* field has two lines.

When a file contains a few records and only one layout, browsing is just a matter of clicking the pages of the Book in the Status Area or dragging the Bookmark.

For a big file, you may have to reduce the file to a reasonable number of records by using the *Find* function in order to browse easily. Sometimes, the designer of the file has included scripts and buttons (see p. 92) to help you locate data.

BEGINNING

The current record is number 1.
The upper page of the Book is empty.
Clicking the lower page would display and activate record number 2.
If a field is active in record 1, the same field is activated in record 2.
The Bookmark is at the top of the Book.
Shortcut: ⌘-Tab displays and activates the next record.

BOOKMARK

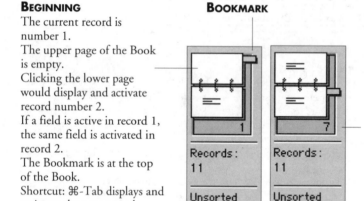

MIDDLE

Current record is number 7.
Clicking the upper page of the Book displays and activates record number 6.
Clicking the lower page displays and activates record number 8.
The Bookmark is a little more than half way down.
Shortcuts: ⌘-Tab displays and activates the next record, Shift-⌘-Tab the preceding one.

END

The current record is number 11.
The lower page of the Book is empty.
Clicking the upper page would display and activate record number 10.
The Bookmark is at the bottom of the Book.
Shortcut: Shift-⌘-Tab displays and activates the preceding record.

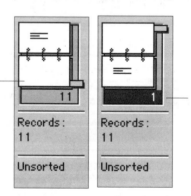

NUMBER

In a big file, with several hundred or thousand records, locating one of them by clicking the pages of the Book would be too slow, and dragging the Bookmark would not be very precise.
To find a record, select the number at the bottom-right of the Book by clicking or by pressing the Escape key, type the number of the record you need, and press the Return or Enter key to display it.

Whether a file is *Viewed as List* or not, you can browse by using the book or one of the keyboard shortcuts given on the opposite page; this displays and activates a record.

When the file is *Viewed as List*, you can also change the record on display by scrolling; the active record may then move out of sight. See how to display it below.

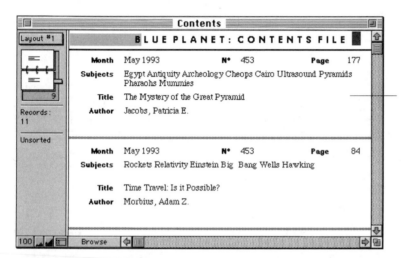

SCROLLED

There is no doubt that this file has been scrolled with the scroll bar: the Book says that the current record is number 9, but records 1 and 2 are displayed on screen. Clicking the top or bottom page of the Book would display record 8 or 10; clicking the other page would then return the display to number 9. See another method below.

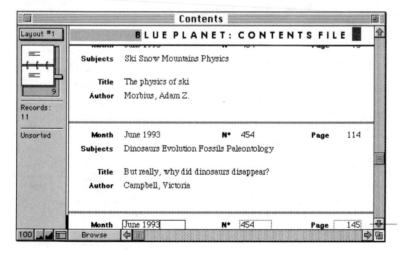

CURRENT

Pressing the Tab key displays the top of the current record by activating its first field.

If the designer of the file has created several different formats for displaying data, or *layouts,* you can choose a layout name in the pop-up menu at the top of the Status Area. This is a very powerful feature of FileMaker Pro.

The data does not change when you switch from one layout to another, but some of it may be hidden. The layout on the opposite page, for example, does not show the *Number* and *Page* fields.

LAYOUT #1

Layout #1 is a default name.
You can name a layout when you create it, or rename it later; this is done in Layout mode.
You can create as many different layouts as disk space allows.

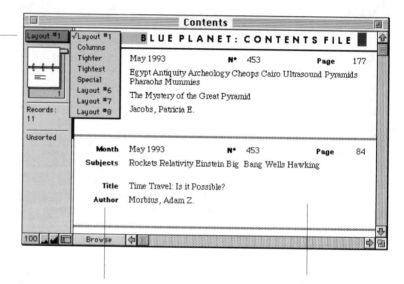

LABELS

Header and Field labels (e.g., *Month, Subjects,* etc.) are just layout scenery.
The designer can decide that they'll disappear when you switch to another layout.
A field can also disappear. If it is retained, it will contain the same data when you switch layout, although its shape or location may change.

DATA ENTRY

You need a basic layout such as this one (which you might name *Data Entry*) to enter data.
In our example, it is the only Layout showing the *Number* and *Page* fields, so you can't enter these data into other Layouts.

Change Layout

The *Columns* layout below is designed for the *Blue Planet* editors' daily use: they want to know which month an article was published, but they don't need the issue number or the page.

The *Tighter* layout (see p. 20) is a variant of *Columns,* used for printing a list of "found" articles about a certain subject.

The *Tightest* layout (p. 21) is for the Publisher, who likes to see a list of several years' articles.

COLUMNS
In this type of layout, the fields are aligned in vertical columns.

HEADER
In a *Columns* layout, field labels appear only once, inside the header.
This saves a lot of space.

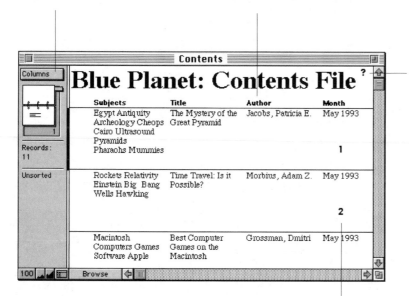

QUESTION MARK
When the file is printed, this question mark becomes a page number (see Preview, p. 73). You must go to Layout mode to insert or change such a sign.

AUTO-ENTRY
Although you enter all data into Layout #1 (see opposite page), Layout #1 does not have to show all the fields. For example, the *Columns* layout shows a new field: the record number. However, this number is not entered by hand, but is an *Auto-Entry.* See p. 44.

The layout shown on the preceding pages simply uses the space available in the window—in this example, a 9-inch screen.

You may want to use a wider layout when the list is printed, to use the full width of the paper sheet. In that case, part of the layout will be hidden outside the window, as in the first picture below. You can display the whole layout by hiding the Status Area (second picture).

On a 14-inch screen, you can see the functional width of a page, but if you want to see the margins (in Preview mode— see p. 73), you still have to hide the Status Area.

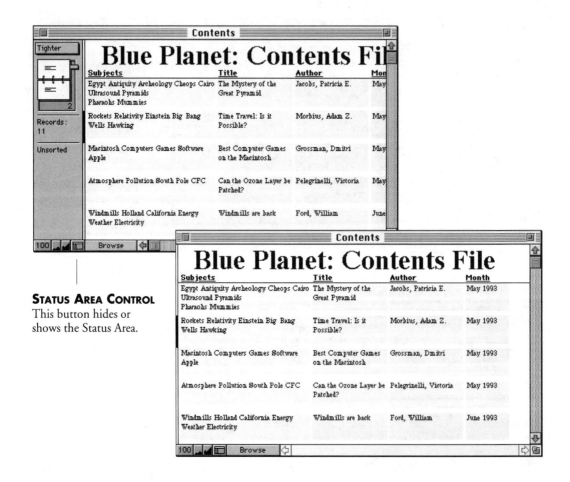

STATUS AREA CONTROL
This button hides or shows the Status Area.

Another way to display more data is to write it in smaller type. For example, you could print a long list of articles in 9 pt Times. It's hard to read on screen at 100%, but FileMaker Pro lets you zoom closer; once printed on a LaserWriter, it is quite readable.

The zoom feature is actually more useful when you design a layout and need to shape and align fields and graphics precisely.

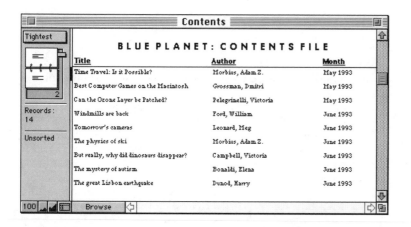

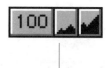

ZOOM CONTROLS
Click the big mountain to zoom in, and the small one to zoom out. Possible percentages are 25, 50, 100, 200 and 400%. Clicking the *Zoom percentage box* when it shows any percentage but 100 returns it to 100. Clicking it when it shows 100 changes the scale to the previous one; you can "toggle" between 100 and another scale by clicking repeatedly.

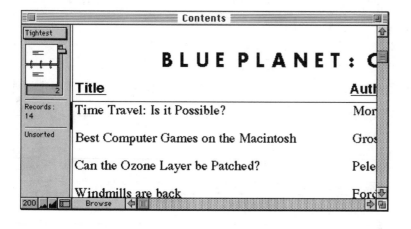

21

Once you have entered the data, "finding" is the main task you would use FileMaker for at *Blue Planet:* you must find all the articles written about a certain subject—or, as in the example below, written by a certain author.

You go to *Find* mode by choosing **Find** in the **Select** menu or in the *Mode* pop-up menu at the bottom of the window, or by typing ⌘-**F**. Then you write the criteria you want in the *Subjects* or *Author* field, and click the *Find* button or press the Return or Enter key.

The program extracts from the file all the records containing the wanted criteria. This is different from word processing programs, where the *Find* feature finds words.

CRITERIA

Here, the goal is to retrieve the set of records containing "Morbius" in the *Author* field.

When you switch to Find mode, a blank record appears. Just write the search criteria into the field you wish to search.

The search would work as well if "morb" were written here. The beginning of the word is what counts: nothing would be found if "bius" was entered as criteria.

Case does not matter: "morb," "Morb," and "MORB" are okay.

REQUEST

The blank record including the criteria to be found is called a request.

The **Refind** command in the **Select** menu displays the last request.

OMIT

When this box is checked, the search is turned on its head: the records with the criteria are *excluded* from the found set.

SYMBOLS

This button opens a pop-up menu which lets you elaborate on the default search. See p. 24.

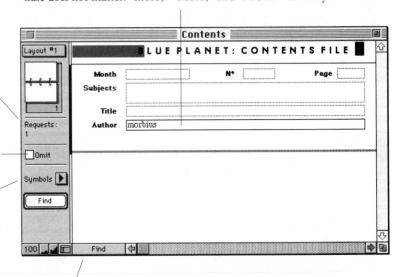

FIND MODE

The name of the active mode appears in the Mode Selector.

Two articles by Adam Z. Morbius were found. The file is now apparently reduced to this "found set." The found records can be printed or sorted, and their spelling can be checked; browsing will not display any other record. The *Find* feature, however, will still search for criteria through the whole file.

To go back to the complete file, you must choose **Find all** in the **Select** menu, or press ⌘-**J**.

CRITERIA

All the records of the found set contain "Morbius" in their Author field. They would also be found if the name was written Adam Z. Morbius.

FOUND

The file is now quite similar to a file with only two records. You know that it is a found set, however, because the Status Area says *Found: 2*.
It may happen that the found set contains nearly the whole file, say 9 records out of 11, and that you forget it is a found set.
Then you panic because you're afraid two records have disappeared.
Just choose **Find all** to display the complete file again.

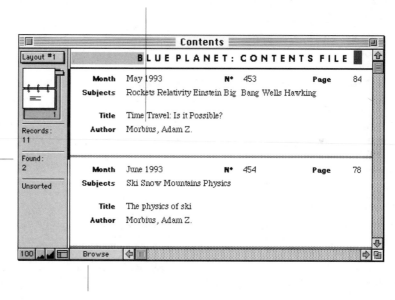

BROWSE

The Status Area of the *Find* mode vanishes when the search is over, and the program returns to Browse mode.

The *Symbols* pop-up menu of the Find Status Area lets you go beyond the simple search described on the preceding pages.

Actually, when you choose one of the commands, the symbol it begins with is entered automatically into the selected field. You get exactly the same result by typing the symbol yourself from the keyboard into the field.

```
<   less than
≤   less than or equal
>   greater than
≥   greater than or equal
=   exact match
... range
!   duplicates
//  today's date
?   invalid date or time
@   one character
*   zero or more characters
""  literal text
```

< LESS THAN, ETC.
Entering "<454" into the *Number* field of our example will find all the records with a number smaller than 454.
The sign ≤ (which you can get by typing Option and <) means "smaller than or equal to."
These signs also work with dates and words. Searching "<Morbius" finds the records where the *Name* field begins with letters A to Mor.

= EXACT MATCH
Looking for "morb" will find "Morbius."
Looking for "=morb" will find only "morb" (or "Morb," "MORB," etc.).
Looking for "=" finds empty fields.

... RANGE
"Find a…b" means "find a and b and everything in between"; a and b can be words in a text field, numbers in a number field, or dates in a date field.

! DUPLICATES
Enter the exclamation point alone into the field; the program then finds all the records with duplicate entries in this field.
For example, putting an exclamation point into the *Author* field of our small file will find the records of regular contributors, like Morbius or Campbell, and exclude one-shot stringers.
You might also check whether records have not been entered twice by mistake.

// TODAY
This should be entered into a date field to find all the records with today's date.

? INVALID DATE OR TIME
You can search for records with unlawful date (e.g. 2/29/1994) or time inside date or time fields.

@ ONE CHARACTER
Looking for "m@rb" will find "Morbius." This is called a "wildcard" search.

* ZERO OR MORE CHARS
Looking for "m*s" or "*bius" will also find Morbius.

LITERAL
Complete words entered into fields are indexed by FileMaker Pro. This accelerates finding, since the program does not sift the whole file, but only the index.
Literal Text lets you find characters that are not indexed, like "," and "Z," as well as groups of words like "Big Bang." You could also type a hard space (Option-Space) between Big and Bang to make it one word in the index.

Find: Advanced

In the first example below, several *criteria* are entered to get all the articles Morbius wrote about snow. Thus, the search is for the criteria [Morbius *and* snow].

In the second example, several *requests* are created to find all the articles by Morbius plus all the articles by Campbell, i.e., search for the criteria [Morbius *or* Campbell].

You can also search for [(Morbius *and* snow) *or* Campbell], and other combinations.

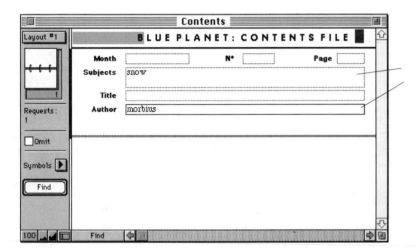

SEVERAL CRITERIA
The criteria can be in the same or in different fields, and can include the symbols mentioned on the opposite page, such as <, >, and so on.

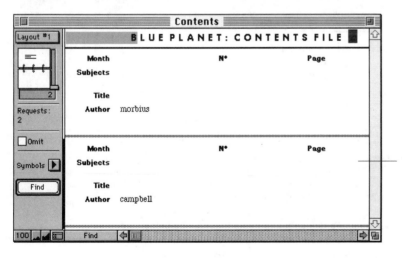

SEVERAL REQUESTS
In the *Find* mode, the **Edit** menu includes a **New Request** command in place of **New Record**. You can have as many simultaneous requests as you want, and enter criteria whichever legitimate way you like. Use the Book or the scroll bar to browse through the requests.

25

Choosing the **Sort...** command in the **Select** menu displays the dialog box below.

At first the right side is empty. Selecting the name of a field on the left and clicking *Move* copies it over to the right side. This has been done for *Author* and *N°* below, which means that the sort will rank the records in alphabetical order of authors and that the various articles by one author will be ranked by the *Blue Planet* issue in which they were published.

Note that whenever a *Move* button exists in a FileMaker Pro dialog box, you can double-click a name to move it.

MOVE AND CLEAR
When you select an item on the right, the *Move* button becomes *Clear*.

DOUBLE ARROW
When you move the pointer over this double arrow, it takes a double-arrow shape. You can then drag items up or down. Here, you might change the Sort Order.

ENGLISH
This pop-up menu gives you a choice of various alphabetical orders. For example, you can choose *Swiss French* or *Swiss German*, etc. In case you really want to know: *Swiss German* probably has a ß letter (no refund if this is not the right answer).

FIELD LIST
Even when some fields are hidden in the active layout, you see a complete list of fields here; thus, you can sort by hidden fields.

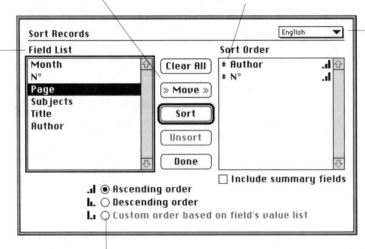

CUSTOM ORDER
Sorting by the *Month* field of our example in ascending order would give you a silly result: April, August, December, etc.

To circumvent the alphabetical order, you might attach a "value list" to the field (see p. 45), and put "January, February, etc." in this list. Then a sort based on the value list will rank the records according to the regular order of the months.

Another way to proceed is to create a date field for the month (with "Oct 91" as date format—see p. 89). Sorting by this field will also rank the *Blue Planet* records by the regular order of the months.

If the author names were entered as Adam Z. Morbius, Elena Bonaldi, and Victoria Campbell, sorting the file by the *Author* field would rank the records not by the authors' surnames, but by their first names. If you ever plan to sort a file by names, you should either put surnames and first names in different fields, or write the surname first as in the example below.

Similarly, if you are sorting by months according to a values list (see opposite page), the month should have a field to itself, with the year in a separate field.

HIDDEN

When the file is sorted by authors, Bonaldi comes before Campbell. As there are two Campbell records, they are sorted by the hidden *N°* field: the May article (#453) comes before the June one (#454). Since it is quite possible that someone writes several articles in the same issue, it makes sense to have three successive sort criteria: *Author, N°,* and *Page.*

SORTED

The file does not shrink to something like a "found set": it is complete, with the records in a different order.

A click on *Unsort* in the Sort dialog box brings back the original order.

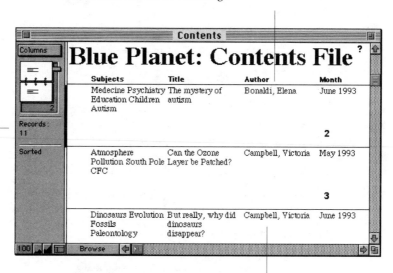

WRONG AUTHOR

Let's say there was a mistake: Adam Z. Morbius, not Vicky Campbell, wrote the dinosaur article after seeing Jurassic Park. If his name is entered in place of hers, the Status Area says *Semi-sorted*, as the order is not correct anymore.

Choosing the **Sort** command and clicking the *Sort* button would move the record to its new correct location.

If you want the *Find* and *Sort* features to perform smoothly, you must be very careful *(i.e., v-e-r-y c-a-r-e-f-u-l)* about the spelling of the words.

Suppose that you are a *Swiss French* librarian at Blue Planet, and occasionally use a French spelling for an English word. This didn't matter when you had to find paper files that you prepared yourself, but now, if you type "medecine," a journalist trying to locate articles about medicine won't find anything.

The best way to avoid this situation is to use the wonderful Claris *Spell as you type* option. The computer will beep whenever you type an unknown word.

CHECK

The **Spelling** command of the **Edit** menu lets you check all the records that can be reached (the "found set"), or a selection of text, or one record. Here, the first record visible on p. 27 is spell-checked.

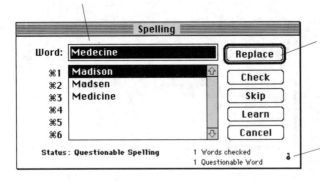

REPLACE

You can accept the program's suggestion or select another suggestion, or enter a spelling yourself (which you may check).

CONTEXT

Clicking this little flag displays a box with the word in context, as can be seen on the opposite page for "Bonaldi."

BEEP

Even if you are a spelling bee laureate, you might use this feature to detect typing errors. Its only drawback is that it slows the program a little.

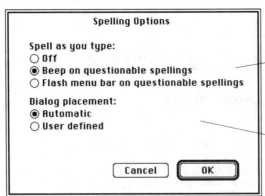

DIALOG PLACEMENT

If you move the dialog box to your favorite corner and check *User defined*, it will always appear there.

The program checks spelling by looking for typed words in two dictionaries: the *Main Dictionary*, which obviously doesn't know proper nouns like Bonaldi, and the *User Dictionary*, which will know such nouns or any other word (for example, foreign) that you add to it by clicking the *Learn* button.

You can have several main dictionaries (for different languages) and user dictionaries (for different domains).

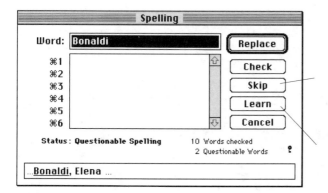

SKIP

If you never make mistakes, you won't have to replace words, but the program will nevertheless stop at most proper nouns. Keep the pointer above this button and click to go to the next "questionable spelling."

When you skip a word, the program is clever enough to go on skipping it throughout the current spell check.

LEARN

When you click this button, the unknown word is added to the *User Dictionary* (although you don't see this happen), and it ceases to be "questionable."

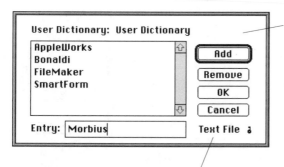

USER DICTIONARY

Choosing the **User Dictionary...** command displays the contents of the dictionary (you can't do that with the main dictionary).

The default user dictionary contains only three words. "Bonaldi" was added when the *Learn* button was clicked.

It is possible to add words directly in the *Entry* box; it makes sense to do so for Morbius and the magazine's other regular contributors.

TEXT FILE

Clicking the flag shows two more buttons: *Import* and *Export*. If the list of regular contributors already exists as a "Text only" (ASCII) file, it is easier to import it whole than to type the names one by one into the *Entry* box.

29

There are two types of pictures in the example below.

The map was pasted in *Layout* mode. In this mode, it is an "object" (see p. 48) that can be selected with a click, dragged around, and resized.

The portrait of Dmitri Grossman was imported (with the **Import Picture...** command—see pp. 54 and 64) inside a "picture field." The field was created in *Layout* mode; in *Browse* mode, its borders become visible when you click it or press the Tab key, and a different picture can be imported or pasted for each record—just as the same text field contains a different text when you change the record.

SCRAPBOOK

This map was copied in the Scrapbook and pasted in Layout mode onto the Header. You can also paste a picture-object in the middle of a record in Layout mode. It then appears in the middle of all the records in Browse mode.

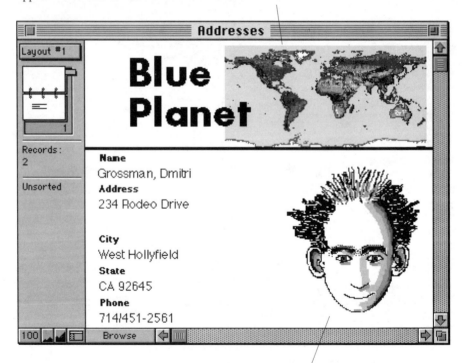

FORMAT

Most drawing and scanned picture formats for the Macintosh can be imported or pasted. You can also import QuickTime movies and paste Macintosh sounds into a Picture field. Double-click the field to play the sounds. See p. 64.

Pictures

Select a picture field in the *Layout* mode and choose the **Picture Format...** command in the **Format** menu to see the dialog box below. Once a picture format has been chosen, all the different pictures that belong to the picture field in the different records are resized or cropped according to the format.

The cropped part of a picture is not destroyed: you can see it again by changing the picture format.

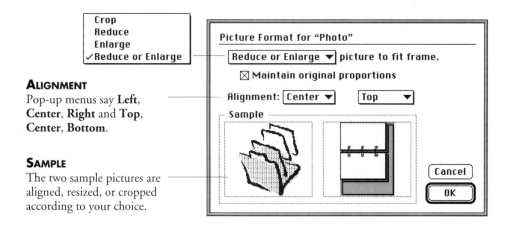

ALIGNMENT
Pop-up menus say **Left**, **Center**, **Right** and **Top**, **Center**, **Bottom**.

SAMPLE
The two sample pictures are aligned, resized, or cropped according to your choice.

CROP
The picture is not resized.

MAINTAIN PROPORTIONS
Default options are *Reduce or Enlarge* and *Maintain original proportions*.
In this example, the program reduces the picture to fit the field while maintaining proportions.

FIT FRAME
If *Maintain original proportions* is not checked, the programs fits the picture into the frame by lengthening the face. In some cases, the *Reduce* and *Enlarge* options give you two different ways to fit the frame.

31

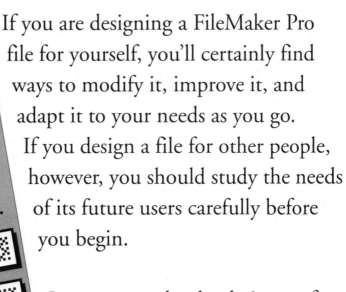

If you are designing a FileMaker Pro file for yourself, you'll certainly find ways to modify it, improve it, and adapt it to your needs as you go.
If you design a file for other people, however, you should study the needs of its future users carefully before you begin.

In our example, the designer of the *Blue Planet* files had to interview the librarian at length about the wooden cabinets' filing system.

Oh, by the way: in this section you should identify with the designer. The librarian is now your client!

The Blue Planet *Contents* file is shown on pages 14 and 15 in Browse mode. Choosing the **Layout** command in the **Select** menu or in the Mode pop-up menu at the bottom of the window displays the Layout below.

The data is gone, and only a shell is left. The Status Area is full of tools that can be used to draw graphic objects on any part of the layout (these tools are described on p. 44).

Any change made in *Layout* mode applies to all the records as soon as you go back to *Browse* mode.

PARTS

The default layout has three parts: Header, Body and Footer.

An empty part can be deleted by dragging the part label up to the next part. Here, the Footer has been suppressed in this way.

More about parts on p. 37.

PART LABEL

Moving a *part label* up or down resizes the part.

You can't drag a part label up when items (objects or fields) are in the way; you should move or resize the items first. You can Option-drag, however. This resizes two adjacent parts (when possible), so that an object may leave a part and enter the next one.

FIELDS

The name inside the field is the one given when the field is defined. You can't change it unless you re-define the field (see p. 40); it doesn't appear in *Browse* mode.

The "label" outside the field is at first simply the field's name; it can be changed with the text tool. For example, the label of the *Subjects* field could be changed to "Keywords." Labels are "layout text" or "Text objects" which appear on all the records in *Browse* mode.

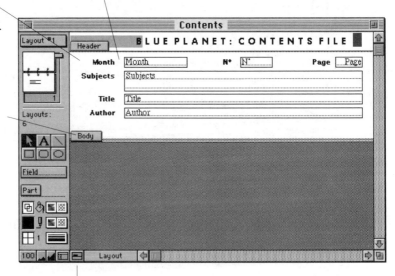

PART LABEL CONTROL

When you click this icon, the part labels switch to a vertical position or back to horizontal.

Vertical part labels can be seen on p. 39; they let you draw or write all the way to the corners of the layout. You need horizontal part labels if you want to resize parts by dragging (you could also use the *Size* palette—see p. 75).

Layout Mode

It can be dangerous to let users go freely to Layout mode: they might delete a field, etc. See p. 58 for how to restrict access.

In our example, you may give the librarian, as a privileged user, full access to all the features of FileMaker Pro. He or she could thus make the simple changes described below.

TEXT OBJECT
When you click an object to select it, four *handles* appear. You can drag the object to move it around.

A text object is special. You can drag its handles horizontally to change its width. To change its height, however, you must choose the **Line Spacing** command in the **Format** menu.

You can fill a text object with a color and give it a border (see p. 46).

FIELD
In Layout mode, a field is an object with handles. You can move it and resize it, or give it a color and a border.

The sample word that appears inside the field shows the default format of the field's text as defined in Layout mode.

Note that you can change the font, size, style and color of selected text in Browse mode, but not its alignment or line spacing.

BASELINE
While you drag an object, you only see a dotted rectangle.

For fields and text objects, a dotted line representing the *baseline* of the text helps you align the text.

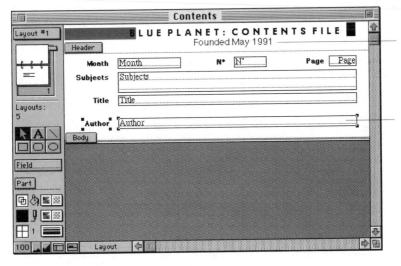

LAYOUT TEXT
Editors would often search for articles published before the creation of the database, so its birth date was added to the Header with the Text tool (see p. 45).

SELECT
The *Author* field label and field were selected together (by dragging a selection rectangle around them or by shift-clicking), then dragged downward. Now the *Title* field can be enlarged so one more line will show.

35

In Layout mode, the **New Record** command of the Browse mode's **Edit** menu is replaced by **New Layout**. The shortcut is still ⌘-**N**. Choosing the command displays the dialog box below.

When you create a brand new file, the first step is not to choose a layout, but to create and name fields (see p. 42). A record in the standard layout is then displayed in Browse mode. You must go to Layout mode to change the layout or create a new one.

A privileged user like *Blue Planet*'s librarian could be allowed to create a new layout. There is no risk of data loss.

LAYOUT TYPE

Seven layout types are available.
Blank is similar to *Standard*, but without any field or label. You might add labels with the Text tool, and fields with the *Field* tool—see p. 42.
Single page form is a one-page Standard layout without a Header or Footer.
See p. 38 for description of other types.
Note that the **Layout Options...** command of the **Layout** menu lets you change a Layout's name.
See p. 79.

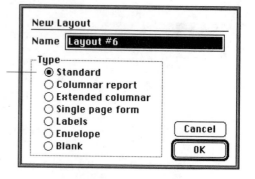

STANDARD

This is a standard layout. Fields and labels can be dragged and resized.
You can change the default fonts, Helvetica 9 pt for labels and Helevetica 12 pt for fields.
Objects can be created here or pasted from another document, and dragged onto the Header, the Body and the Footer.
See also **Layout** and **Arrange** menus (pp. 74 and 80).

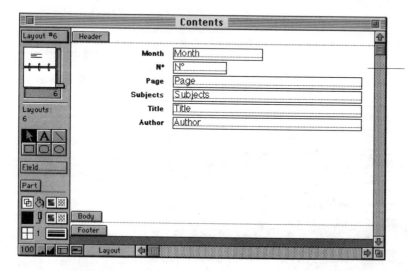

A standard layout has three parts: Header, Body and Footer. You can add more parts, such as Title Header or Sub-Summary, by dragging the *Part Tool* from the Status Area to where you want the part to be on the layout; this displays the *Part Definition* dialog box below. Another method is described on p. 78.

To delete a part, select its label and press the Delete key. If you press Option and Delete, objects in the deleted part move to the part below. To delete an empty part, drag its label up to the next part.

PART TOOL ———

TITLE HEADER OR FOOTER

You can have only one of these, on the first page. It replaces the normal Header or Footer and can be seen only in Preview mode. If you make it large enough, no record will appear on the page.

SUMMARY PART

This type of part is necessary only when you have Summary fields, which sum data on several records (see p. 104).

PRINT OPTIONS

You might want:
A page break (a new page) before a Grand Summary part.
A page break after every *x* records (an option for a Body part).
A new number—i.e., 1—after a Title Header.
When you allow records to be broken across page boundaries, the last option becomes available.

DIMMED

Options are dimmed or highlighted according to what parts already exist (e.g., you can have only one Header, one Body, one Footer) and where you have dragged the *Part* tool.

Part Definition

○ Title Header
○ Header
○ Leading Grand Summary
○ Body
◉ Sub-Summary when sorted by:
○ Trailing Grand Summary
○ Footer
○ Title Footer

Month
N°
Page
Subjects
Title
Author

☐ Page break before each occurrence
☐ Page break after every ⬚ occurrences
☐ Restart page numbers after each occurrence
☐ Allow part to break across page boundaries
　☐ Discard remainder of part before new page

[Cancel]
[OK]

Whereas the default *(Standard)* layout displays all the available fields (which you can delete if you want), choosing *Columnar report, Extended columnar, Labels* or *Envelope* in the *New Layout* dialog box opens a new dialog box, "Set Field Order," which lets you pick up some fields and ignore others.

The example below shows how the "Tighter" *Columnar report* layout on p. 16 was made.

FIELD LIST
This is the list of available fields.
You can define them when you create the file, or add them later.

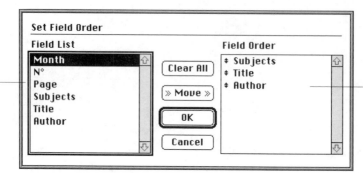

FIELD ORDER
Fields are selected in the Field List and transferred here with the *Move* button or by double-clicking.

COLUMNAR REPORT
This is what the layout looks like after the *Month* field is added to the Field Order in the dialog box above and the *OK* button is clicked.
For the final layout, shown on p. 19, the Body part and the fields were enlarged, the labels were lowered, and 48 pt layout text was written inside the Header.

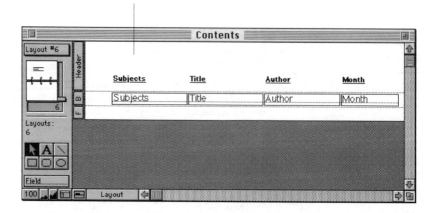

If you want a *Columnar report* layout to look good on a page, you'd better limit the number of fields. Otherwise, the program will give you a layout that is not really columnar, as in the first picture below.

The second picture shows an *Extended columnar* layout, in which fields stay on one line, extending beyond the screen.

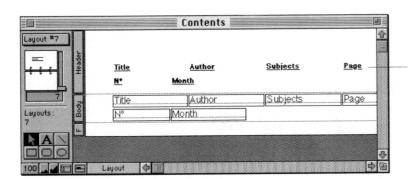

COLUMNAR REPORT
When all the fields in our example are included, the program "wraps" field labels and fields like this.

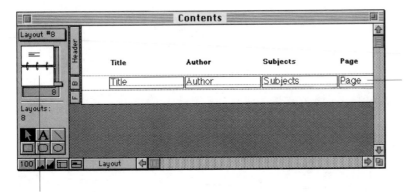

EXTENDED COLUMNAR
Field labels and fields stay on one line, but they extend beyond the screen and possibly beyond the paper page.
You can start from such a layout and improve it: the width of the *Page*, *N°* and *Month* fields could be reduced; Helvetica 12 could be replaced by the much smaller Times 10. You might also change the paper width or page orientation in the *Page Setup* dialog box (see p. 62) to give yourself more space.

BOOK
Notice that in Layout mode, clicking the Book's pages or dragging the Bookmark lets you display layouts. This is more convenient than the Layout pop-up menu.
For example, to explore an unknown file (e.g., a commercial *Template*—see p. 116), you might go to Layout mode and click the Book's lower page (or press ⌘-Tab) to view successive layouts.

When you choose *Labels* in the *New Layout* dialog box, the *Label Setup* dialog box below is displayed first. Clicking OK then opens the *Set Field Order* dialog box.

Choosing *Envelope* in the New Layout dialog box displays the Set Field Order dialog box without passing through Label Setup. The body of the record is sized like an envelope, with a large header. Fields contain tiny characters, like a label stuck onto the envelope.

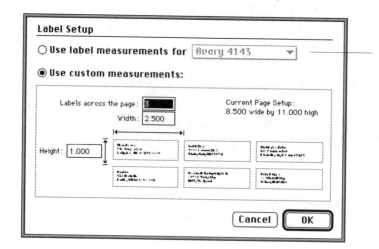

LABEL SETUP

The *Use label measurements* button is checked by default, so that you can choose an Avery label size in the pop-up menu.
Measurements and other particulars of Avery labels can be found in Appendix C of FileMaker Pro user's guide.
When you want to design custom labels, as above, you must remember that the numbers do not measure the labels, but the labels *plus* the distance between them—an important distinction if you want the labels to print precisely on a label sheet.
Labels are set in columns. This is different from *Columnar report*. See p. 79.
See also p. 84 for how to "slide" objects to improve the look of labels and addresses on envelopes.

A *Label* layout shows only one label (first picture below).

In Browse mode, you also see labels one at a time, or one under another as a list (second picture).

Preview mode (third picture) shows them exactly as they should look when printed. You may still be surprised when you print, however—a little trial-and-error fine-tuning is often necessary.

FIELDS

Default fields for labels come in 9 pt Helvetica, without layout text labels.

You can resize these fields and add more by dragging the *Field Tool* from the Status Area (see next page).

The choices of the *Label Setup* dialog box don't bind you forever: you can change the label size in Layout mode by dragging the right border of the label and the *Body* part label.

It is also possible to change the number of labels across by choosing the **Layout Options...** command (see p. 79).

SLID

Notice how data have "slid" closer together from Browse to Preview: the program suppresses the white space inside fields. See p. 84.

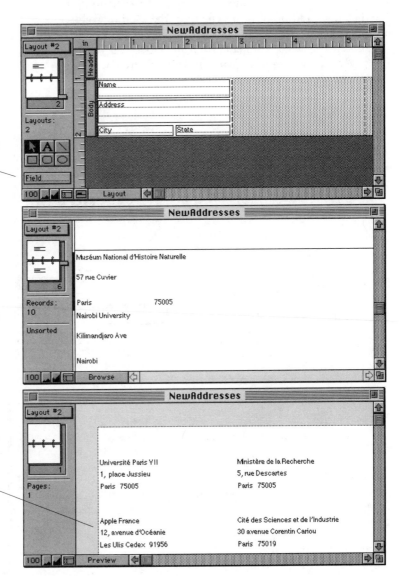

BASICS DESIGNER

When you create a brand new file by double-clicking the FileMaker Pro icon or by choosing **New...** in the **File** menu, the program displays the *Define Fields* dialog box, which is empty at first. To define fields for your file, choose a type for field #1, name it, adjust options if necessary, click *Create*; repeat for field #2, 3, etc. Click *Done* when you have defined all your fields.

Later, you can always define more fields, change definitions, delete fields, or add options, by choosing the **Define Fields...** command in the **Select** menu—which displays the same dialog box. You can access this command from any mode, but you must go to Layout mode if you want to adjust the fields' size, design, location, etc.

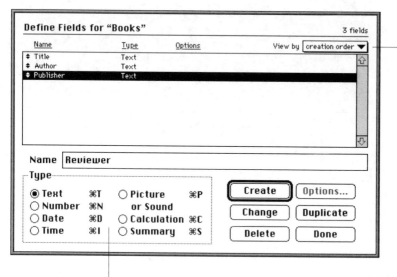

VIEW BY
This Pop-up menu lets you view field names by **creation order**, **field name**, **field type**, or **custom order**.
You can also change the order of field names by dragging the double arrow symbols up or down.

TYPE
Numbers will be treated as text in a Text field, and as numbers in a Number field. The maximum number of characters in a Number field is 255.
Date/Time fields will accept only valid dates/times.
See a Picture field on p. 30, a Calculation field on p. 103, and a Summary field on p. 104.

FIELD TOOL
When you create a field by dragging the *Field Tool* from the Status Area to the layout, this dialog box lets you choose an available field.

Default fonts for fields and field labels are Helvetica 12 and Helvetica 9 bold. You can change the fonts of selected fields and labels in *Layout* mode by pulling down the **Font** submenu of the **Format** menu. See also p. 87.

Whatever you write in a new record's fields in Browse mode will adopt the fields' default font, style, and size, but you can then select any part of the text and change its format (see Browse mode example below).

LAYOUT TEXT

The word "BOOKS" was written with the Text tool over a dark rectangle, and made white with the **Text Color** command of the **Format** menu.

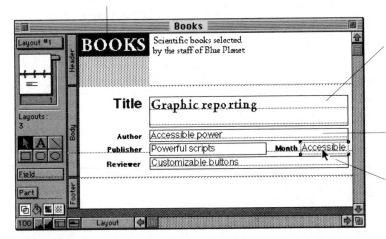

FONT
The font for the *Title* field is 18 pt Garamond Bold.

SAMPLE
Choosing **Sample Data** in the **Layout** menu puts FileMaker Pro marketing claims into the fields so you can see how the text will look.

DOTTED
As the *Month* field is being moved, a dotted baseline helps place it precisely.

BROWSE MODE
The first line of the title is 18 pt Garamond Bold (default font).
The second line was selected and changed to 12 pt Garamond Plain. Note that you'd better stick to Times if you want your file to look good in a Windows environment —where Garamond may be unknown.

43

When a field's name is selected in the *Define Fields* dialog box (see p. 42), either just after it has been created or when you choose the **Define Fields...** command, the *Options...* button is highlighted and you can customize the field.

✓Creation Date
 Creation Time
 Modification Date
 Modification Time
 Creator Name
 Modifier Name

AUTO-ENTER

You can choose data (here, the name of a book reviewer, Barbara Porter) to be included inside the field in every new record.
The *serial number* option lets you number the records. The field must be a number field. See examples of numbered records on pp. 21 and 73. Modification of an auto-entered value can be allowed or prohibited.

DATE, NAME

A field with *Creation Date/Time* as auto-entry lets you know when it was created; a field with *Modification Date/Time* indicates when it was changed.
Creator/Modifier Name refers to the name of the Mac in System 7's Sharing Setup feature.

MORE OPTIONS

See opposite page for *pre-defined value list*. Repeating fields are explained on pp. 90 and 100, Lookup fields and values on p. 106.

Entry Options for Text Field "Reviewer"

Auto-enter a value that is
☐ the [Creation Date ▼]
☐ a serial number:
next value [1]
increment by [1]
☒ data [Barbara Porter]

Verify that the field value is
☐ not empty
☐ unique ☐ an existing value
☐ of type [Number ▼] ✓Number
                       Date
                       Time
☐ from [   ]
    to [   ]

☐ Prohibit modification of auto-entered values
☐ Repeating field with a maximum of [2] values
☒ Use a pre-defined value list: [Edit Values...]
☐ Look up values from a file: [Set Lookup...]

[Cancel]
[OK]

VERIFY

Let's say the *not empty* option is checked for the *Publisher* field. When you leave a record without entering data into the field, the alert box at left appears and the computer beeps. *Unique* means there are no other records with the same value in this field. *An existing value* means just the opposite.
Restricting values to a range is possible for Text, Number, Date and Time fields.

⚠ "Publisher" is defined to require a value. Allow this field to remain empty?

[Cancel] [OK]

This example shows the making of a *pre-defined value list*.

This kind of list saves a lot of time—and prevents errors—if you have to repeatedly enter values from a fixed list, such as names of book reviewers (see below).

DISPLAY VALUES

Clicking the *Edit Values…* button in the *Entry Options* dialog box opens this dialog box, where you enter the values (here, *Blue Planet*'s usual book reviewers).

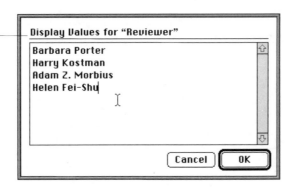

VALUE LIST

This is the default "Pop-up list" display. It pops up when the field is active. You can select one of the suggested names by clicking or by pressing the Up and Down keyboard arrows; pressing Enter or double-clicking puts the value into the field. You can also ignore the list's suggestions and type something else.

The **Field Format…** command in the **Format** menu lets you choose the other display types (see p. 90).

POP-UP MENU

You can choose a reviewer in the pop-up menu. Note that this traditional Macintosh pop-up menu does not behave like the pop-up list: no pressing of the Enter key or double-clicking, no scroll bar.

The **Field Format…** command lets you add an *Other…* option.

CHECK BOXES

Several options can be checked.

RADIO BUTTONS

You can check only one option.

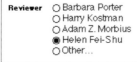

BASICS DESIGNER

The tools below may only be used in *Layout* mode. What you draw or write with them will appear on all the records, either above or below the record (if located in the Header or Footer) or on the record itself.

When you click the line, rectangle/rounded rectangle or oval tool, the pointer takes a crosshair shape. As soon as you finish dragging with this crosshair pointer to create an object, the arrow pointer comes back and the arrow tool is selected again. If you want to keep a tool selected, double-click it.

Note that you can "toggle" between a drawing tool and the arrow tool by pressing the Enter key.

TEXT TOOL

Click anywhere to write layout text. When you select the arrow tool again, the layout text becomes a Text object with handles, which can be dragged around and resized. If you drag the I-beam pointer to define a *bounding box* before writing, the text is constrained by the box.

You get exactly the same result by dragging a handle of an existing Text object.

LINE TOOL

Drag from A to B to draw a straight AB line.

Shift-drag or Option-drag to make it horizontal or vertical (Option also lets you draw 45-degree lines).

ARROW TOOL

The *arrow* or *pointer* tool lets you move and resize objects.

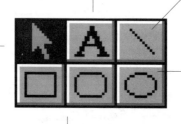

OVAL

Drag from A to B to draw an oval inside rectangle AB. Option-drag to draw a circle.

RECTANGLE/ROUNDED RECTANGLE

Drag from A to B to draw a rectangle or rounded rectangle with AB as diagonal. While in most Macintosh programs, you Shift-drag to draw squares or circles, in FileMaker Pro you must Option-drag.

You can fill selected graphic objects (except lines), fields, and text objects with *fill* colors and patterns. See examples on the next page.

When you select a line or any object except a Text object and choose a *pen* color, pattern, and width, these attributes apply to the line or to the border of the object.

SAMPLES

The first two boxes show the currently selected color and pattern for fill and for lines/borders. The bottom box shows the active line width.

Choosing fill and pen attributes when no object is selected defines "preset" attributes that apply to new objects. You can also define preset attributes *by imitation:* just Command-click an existing object.

Choosing attributes for a selected object does not change the preset attributes applying to new objects.

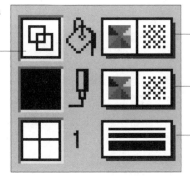

FILL COLOR AND PATTERN

Default fill is transparent.

PEN COLOR AND PATTERN

Default pen color is solid black.

PEN WIDTH

Default width is 1 pt for lines, "None" for other objects.

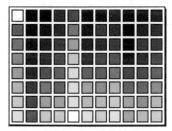

COLOR

This is the 88-color palette for a grayscale or 256-color screen. On a black-and-white Macintosh, the Color pop-up menu shows a limited choice of color *names*, so you can still select a color for an object.

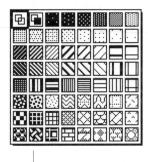

PATTERN

The first pattern is transparent (or "empty"). You don't get a transparent color, but no color. The second pattern is solid color. If you choose a pattern other than solid, the active color applies to the pattern's dots.

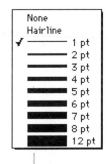

LINE WIDTH

Hairline means 0.25 pt for a LaserWriter printer. It appears on screen as 1 pt at 400% scale, but also at 100%, because screen pixels are 1 pt wide.

To move or modify an object, you must select it by clicking it or by dragging a selection rectangle around the object. If you Command-drag, you don't need to include the whole object inside the selection rectangle.

It is usually possible to modify several objects at the same time after selecting them together. When objects are close to each other, dragging a selection rectangle or Command-dragging is the easiest way to select them. If they are far apart, you can click the first object, then Shift-click the other ones.

The **Select All** command selects all the objects. When a tool is selected, this command selects all the objects created with this tool. You can also select an object or a field, press Option and choose **Select All** to select all the similar objects or all the fields.

OBJECT

This is a typical FileMaker Pro object. Click inside to select it. Drag to move it, or press a keyboard arrow key to move it one pixel at a time. Drag a handle to resize it. The fill is one color, the border another.

TWO TEXT OBJECTS AND A FIELD

The fill of the first text object shows how a color and a pattern combine. Note that a Text object can't have a border.
The fill of the second text object is a solid color. The text is made white with the **Text Color** command of the **Format** menu.
The last object is a field. Its border is a 4 pt black line with a pattern.

SHADOW EFFECT

Here, two similar text objects with a small offset are colored with the **Text Color** command.

THREE BLIND MICE

The first mouse was drawn in HyperCard, then copied, pasted onto a FileMaker Pro layout, and duplicated.
A black-and-white picture like this one can be colored very easily: just select it and choose a pen color. That's how these mice were made.

FileMaker Pro objects and imported graphics can be combined to create effective Headers and layouts.

Designing, sizing, and positioning objects is made somewhat easier by the commands of the **Layout** and **Arrange** menus (see pp. 74 to 85).

If you are a Macintosh beginner, you might try to practice creating graphics in programs like HyperCard or MacDraw Pro. If you want your database to look professional, you might consider asking a serious Macintosh artist to design it.

HEADER

The Header of the *Addresses* file was last seen on p. 30.

The original Scrapbook picture of the world is large. It was reduced—and slightly flattened—by dragging a handle inward.

Shift-dragging resizes in one direction only; Option-dragging resizes proportionately.

The first picture shows five separate objects. In practice, it is not necessary to create them apart from each other like this.

The transparent rectangle with a two-pixel wide gray border can be drawn around the map. The gray rectangle with no border ("line width: none") is drawn in front of the map, with a slight offset, then sent behind (**Send to back** command of the **Arrange** menu, see p. 82).

The two words of the title are different objects. Thus, they can have different colors and be moved separately.

In the third picture, the title gets some depth by being duplicated twice. One duplicate is colored white; the other, dark gray.

Menus

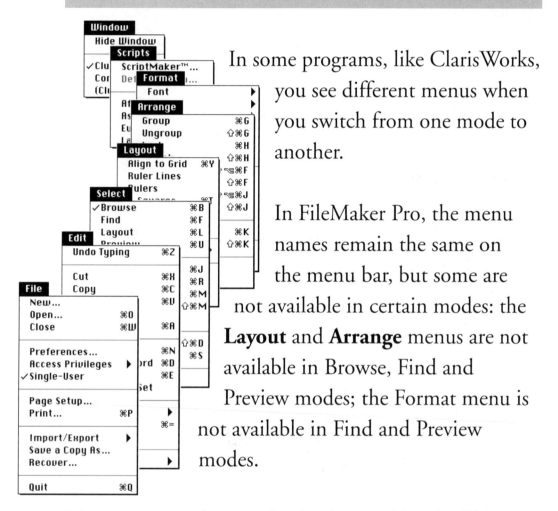

In some programs, like ClarisWorks, you see different menus when you switch from one mode to another.

In FileMaker Pro, the menu names remain the same on the menu bar, but some are not available in certain modes: the **Layout** and **Arrange** menus are not available in Browse, Find and Preview modes; the Format menu is not available in Find and Preview modes.

Menu commands may also be dimmed by the file's designer if he or she wishes to restrict access to certain features. See *Access*, p. 60.

MENUS APPLE

When FileMaker Pro is in use, two commands are added to the **Apple** menu: **About FileMaker Pro...** and **Help...**

If the Help file is not installed, choosing the **Help...** command displays a dialog box asking where Help is located.

ABOUT FILEMAKER PRO
See below.

HELP
See opposite page.

APPLE MENU FOLDER
This picture shows the default commands of the **Apple** menu. System 7 lets you add more commands by dragging files to the *Apple Menu* folder inside the System Folder. For example, you might put aliases of FileMaker Pro *Templates* (see p. 116) in the **Apple** menu.

INFO
The *Info* button displays more detailed information than is usual in this kind of dialog box.
The *Credits* scroll upward like in old-fashioned movies.

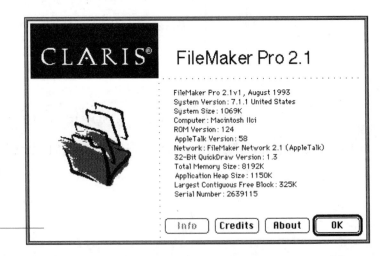

CLARIS®   FileMaker Pro 2.1

FileMaker Pro 2.1v1, August 1993
System Version: 7.1.1 United States
System Size: 1069K
Computer: Macintosh IIci
ROM Version: 124
AppleTalk Version: 58
Network: FileMaker Network 2.1 (AppleTalk)
32-Bit QuickDraw Version: 1.3
Total Memory Size: 8192K
Application Heap Size: 1150K
Largest Contiguous Free Block: 325K
Serial Number: 2639115

[Info] [Credits] [About] [OK]

Help

The FileMaker Pro Help program is a separate HyperCard-type stack of more than two hundred cards, which you can keep open behind your FileMaker Pro window while you work.

It is very useful, and offers all kinds of hypertext and pop-up goodies that this book lacks…

Option-dragging lets you select Help text to copy it as text. Command-dragging lets you select a rectangular part of the screen to copy it as picture. Try it!

NAVIGATION
Sends you to a card that explains what the other buttons are for.

INDEX
Displays an electronic index of FileMaker Pro keywords.

RETRACE
Returns to the last seen card, then to the card seen before that, etc.

PREVIOUS
Takes you to the previous card. Shortcut: left keyboard arrow.

NEXT
Takes you to the next card. Shortcut: right keyboard arrow.

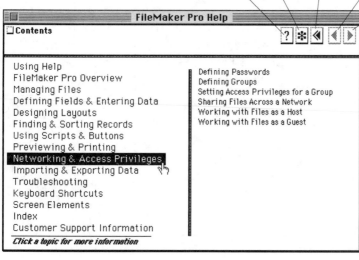

BALLOONS
If you like System 7 Help Balloons, note that they work nicely with window items and menu commands in FileMaker Pro.

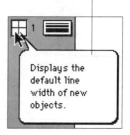

53

File is a universal Macintosh menu which lets you create, open and print documents. You should memorize its shortcuts: ⌘-**O**, ⌘-**W**, ⌘-**P** and ⌘-**Q**.

If you are familiar with other Macintosh programs, you may notice that two basic shortcuts are missing: ⌘-**N** is not used for a new file, but for a new record, request, or layout (**Edit** menu, p. 66). As there is no **Save** command in FileMaker Pro, there is no ⌘-**S** shortcut in this menu.

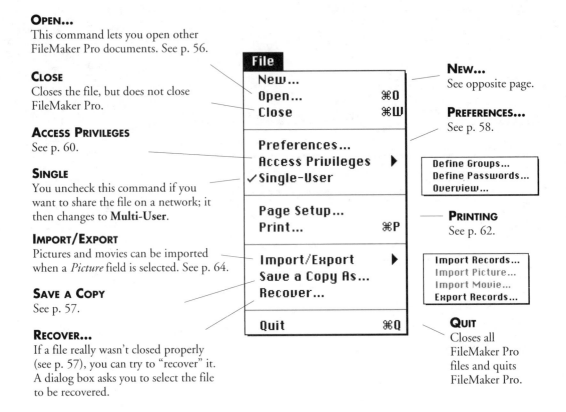

OPEN...
This command lets you open other FileMaker Pro documents. See p. 56.

CLOSE
Closes the file, but does not close FileMaker Pro.

ACCESS PRIVILEGES
See p. 60.

SINGLE
You uncheck this command if you want to share the file on a network; it then changes to **Multi-User**.

IMPORT/EXPORT
Pictures and movies can be imported when a *Picture* field is selected. See p. 64.

SAVE A COPY
See p. 57.

RECOVER...
If a file really wasn't closed properly (see p. 57), you can try to "recover" it. A dialog box asks you to select the file to be recovered.

NEW...
See opposite page.

PREFERENCES...
See p. 58.

PRINTING
See p. 62.

QUIT
Closes all FileMaker Pro files and quits FileMaker Pro.

Choosing the **New...** command starts the three-step process described below. This is only one way to create a new file. You can also duplicate a *Template*—a file with pleasant layouts and formats that you have created as a mother to other files.

FileMaker Pro comes with a series of Templates (see p. 116). You create new files by "cloning" them. Cloning files is not as dangerous as cloning dinosaurs. See p. 57.

NAME THE NEW FILE

This standard dialog box lets you name the file and decide where to save it.

A Macintosh name cannot have more than 31 characters; the character ":" (colon) is forbidden. In a cross-platform situation, you might create Windows-type eight-character names, such as "Books.FM"—the ".FM" ending is required.

Clicking *New...* displays the next dialog box.

DEFINE THE FIELDS

Choose a field type, name the field, and click *Create* for every field you want in your file. See p. 40.

Clicking *Done* displays the file in Browse mode as below.

NEW FILE

The new file has only one record and one standard layout called Layout #1.

You must go to Layout mode if you want to modify this layout or create new ones.

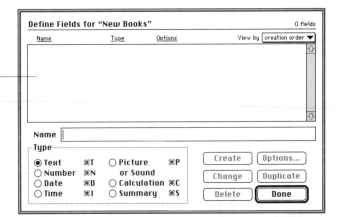

55

When several FileMaker Pro documents are open at the same time (maximum number is fourteen), it is easy to copy data or layout items from one document to another.

Beginners who want to close document *A* and open document *B* often quit the program and double-click the icon of document *B* on the desktop to open it. It is much faster to choose the **Close** command, then display the dialog box below by choosing the **Open...** commands.

FOLDER
The files in the list below are saved in this folder. Clicking its name opens a pop-up menu that shows the hierarchy of folders that contain it; you can "navigate" through the hierarchy by choosing a name in the pop-up menu or by pressing the Command key and the Up or Down Arrow.

VOLUME
The folder belongs to the *Macintosh HD* hard disk. Clicking this icon lets you climb up the folder hierarchy one step at a time.

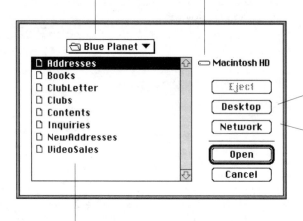

DESKTOP
When you click this button, the list of available volumes —hard disks, floppy disks, Syquest disks, CD-ROMs, etc.—appears in the main box.

NETWORK
Clicking this button starts the FileMaker Pro filesharing process. See p. 106.

LIST
Files and folders contained in the *Blue Planet* folder are ordered alphabetically here.
Typing a letter displays the names beginning with this letter. This useful trick works in most dialog box lists.
Note that you can make your life much easier by naming files and folders carefully. For example, if you want *VideoSales* to begin the list instead of ending it, rename it "@VideoSales."

There is no **Save** command in the **File** menu of FileMaker Pro: modifications are kept in a "file cache," then saved automatically after a while (see p. 59) to the hard disk. If your Macintosh shuts down accidentally or the screen freezes because of some exotic bug, trying to open the document will display a message that it wasn't closed properly and may need some repairs. Unsaved data is then lost. Another consequence of automatic saving is that wrong moves are saved, replacing good stuff with junk before you notice your mistake.

Thus, if you want to minimize worry, choose the **Save a Copy As...** command now and then. See the dialog box below.

BACKUP

If a floppy disk were inserted inside the drive, its name would appear here and you could save the document onto the floppy disk.
This is one of the ways a *backup* of the document can be made.
No important document should ever exist without a backup
(or two—some say three).

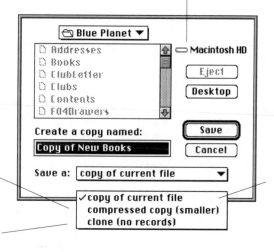

COMPRESSED

A compressed copy takes up less disk space. It is expanded again when you open it.
FileMaker Pro's User Guide calls this an option for archiving and backup, but some authors say that compressing and expanding a big file from time to time makes it leaner and faster.

CLONE

This is a file with the same layouts and fields as the open one, but you see an empty window because the file has no record—and thus, obviously, no data. You create records with the **New Record** command.
Exporting the found set to a clone is a way of reducing the file to the found set.

COPY

This is the same thing as duplicating the file on the desktop.
You might save such a copy before launching some audacious maneuver.

Preferences exist in most Macintosh programs. They let you customize some features of the program.

When the *General* icon at the left of the dialog box is selected, the right section of the dialog box displays as below. It lets you make choices which affect the way you work with all documents, old and new, until you modify General Preferences again.

LOCK LAYOUT TOOLS

By default, a tool stays selected only as long as you keep dragging to create an object, then the Arrow tool is selected again—unless you have selected the tool by double-clicking. Check this box if you want tools to stay selected after you stop dragging.

ADD FIELDS TO LAYOUT

This is checked by default. When you create a new field, it appears in the current layout, and thus in all the records.
If you uncheck this option, you must use the field tool to add a new field to the layout.

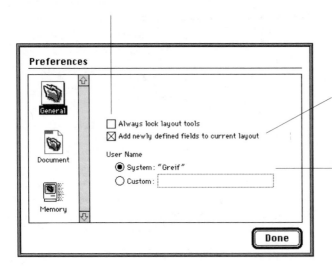

USER NAME

FileMaker Pro lets you enter the *User Name* into fields as an Auto-Entry (see p. 44).
The default name is the one you enter in the *Sharing Setup* control panel of System 7.
If you prefer another name, check *Custom* and write it here.

When the *Document* icon at the left of the dialog box is selected, the right section of the dialog box lets you make choices which affect only the current document.

You may ignore the *Memory* options altogether if you do not use a battery-operated computer such as a PowerBook.

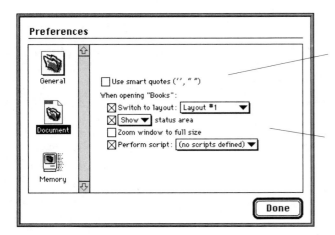

SMART QUOTES

Dumb quotes: "..." and '...'.
Smart quotes: "..." and '...'.
A difference between versions 1.0 and 2.0 of the program: version 1.0 was dumb by default, version 2.0 is smart!

WHEN OPENING

All the boxes are unchecked by default. Three have been checked here to show the pop-up menus.

The first pop-up menu offers a list of the current document's layouts; the third one, a list of its scripts.

The second one says **Show** and **Hide**.
Zoom window to full [screen] size is a good option if the file may travel to other machines, especially in a cross-platform environment.

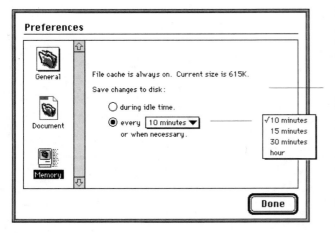

SAVE CHANGES

File cache is where the changes are stored before they are saved to the disk.

Default saving option is *during idle time*. This means "often" and may deplete the battery of a PowerBook. The other option has been chosen here to show its pop-up menu.

"Every 10 minutes" means every 10 minutes or less. It can be less if the file cache is full.

"When necessary" means *as seldom as possible*. This prolongs battery life, but increases the risk of data loss in case of a mishap.

59

MENUS FILE

Blue Planet's wooden file cabinets were kept behind a locked door. FileMaker Pro files must also be locked in some way. Because files can be shared on the network, anybody could modify or destroy them if they were not protected.

Thus, three user groups and four passwords were created. One password is for the designer and the librarian; the others, which allow different levels of access, are for the three groups.

Note that protection may be necessary even for a stand-alone Macintosh, if more than one person uses it.

ACCESS PRIVILEGES

The first two commands of the **Access Privileges** submenu display the dialog boxes below.

Overview... opens the dialog box on the opposite page.

> Define Groups...
> Define Passwords...
> Overview...

GROUPS

You enter names and create groups in this dialog box. This is possible only when the file is set to *Single-User*. Obviously, everyone should know what group they belong to, and the group's password.

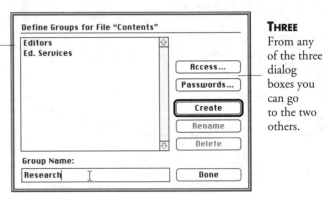

THREE

From any of the three dialog boxes you can go to the two others.

PASSWORDS

This is where you restrict usage of some FileMaker Pro features. Most restrictions result in dimmed menu commands when the *Contents* file is open.

Newton is the designer's and the librarian's password. It allows access to all program features. Such a master password is absolutely necessary: it lets you define and change the other passwords.

Einstein can browse, print, edit and create records.

Curie can only browse and print.

No password will only be able to browse.

Note that Browse represents minimum access and can't be turned off.

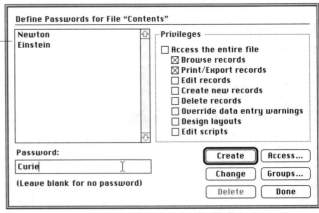

So, you've defined groups and you've defined passwords.

What group uses which password to what purpose is defined in the dialog box below. For example, Editors can open the file with *Einstein,* see all the layouts except #6, and modify the *Subjects, Title, Author,* and *Record Number* fields.

Only the designer and librarian can modify the passwords: the **Access Privileges** command disappears unless the Master password, which accesses the entire file, is entered. For other users, it is replaced by a **Change password...** command, which lets them change their own password.

CHECK

When a group name is selected, the pointer becomes a check sign (✔) over the • bullets.

You can check one or several passwords for a group—but you can't do anything to the Master password, which is special.

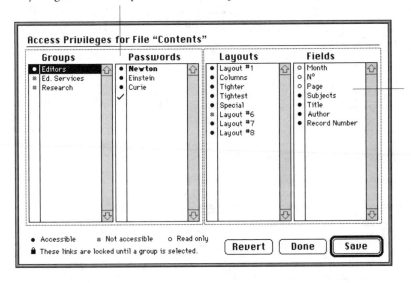

BULLETS

Layout and Field names can be checked into three different states: *Accessible* (black bullet), *Not accessible* (gray bullet) and *Read only* (white bullet).

If editors try to see Layout #6, they get a gray screen with the words *Access denied.*

If you want a certain group not to see some data, put the field containing these data on a forbidden layout.

EINSTEIN

When people try to open the *Contents* file, they are prompted for one of the registered passwords; access to features, layouts and fields depends on the password used. Entering no password lets them only browse the records.

What you write here appears as dots, in case somebody was peeking over your shoulder.

61

The standard Macintosh dialog boxes shown on these two pages offer options for most LaserWriter and StyleWriter printers. Other printers may have slightly different options. Consult your printer's manual.

If your document does not include bitmap text (i.e., pre-TrueType Chicago) and bitmap pictures (MacPaint or TIFF), you can just accept these default settings—and go directly to the opposite page.

PAPER
US Letter: 8.5" x 11". A4 Letter: 8.25" x 11.66".
US Legal: 8.5" x 14". B5 Letter: 8.25" x 12".
The *Tabloid* pop-up menu offers some more special sizes.

REDUCE/ENLARGE
From 25% to 400% (on a regular LaserWriter).

PRINTER EFFECTS
Font Substitution and *Text Smoothing* affect pre-TrueType versions of fonts with city names (e.g., Geneva or New York). You might as well avoid these fonts altogether, because substitution modifies spacing and alignment.
Graphics Smoothing smooths bitmap pictures. Turn it off if you want a sharp rendering of fine details, especially if they are inverted (white on a dark background). Nobody knows what *Faster Bitmap Printing*

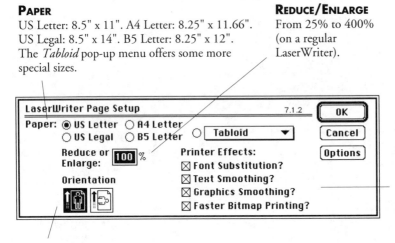

ORIENTATION
Printing sideways is a sensible choice for some columnar report layouts.

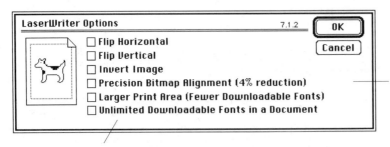

DOWNLOADABLE FONTS
Downloadable fonts are fonts like Garamond, which are not permanent residents of the LaserWriter's memory and are "downloaded" each time they are printed.

OPTIONS
The *Options* button opens this dialog box.
Try *Flip Horizontal, Flip Vertical, Invert Image,* and see what happens to the little dog (some say cow). *Precision Bitmap Alignment* is a must if you print unsmoothed bitmap pictures on a LaserWriter. *Larger Print Area* means a 0.25 inch margin instead of 0.5 inch.

By default, what's printed is the "found set." If you want to print five records out of a ten thousand-record file, you should "find" them before printing. You may also sort records to print them in a certain order. Records print as they appear: they'll be printed one per page if they are viewed one at a time, or several per page if they are viewed as list.

It is a good idea to "preview" your pages before printing (see p. 72), just to be on the safe side.

The print dialog box for a LaserWriter is shown below.

PAGES FROM

The numbers you enter here correspond to *Pages*, which is different from records when records are viewed as list. Preview mode shows pages. Note that to print page 18, you should enter "from 18 to 18." You can print from the beginning or to the end of the file by leaving one of the boxes empty.

PAGE NUMBER

Write "##" as layout text (on the layout) to number pages.
See also p. 71.

DEFAULT PRINTING

Records being browsed means "the found set."

CURRENT RECORD

Prints one record. Can be more than one page.

LaserWriter   "Personal LaserWriter NT"   B1-7.0   **Print**

Copies: **1**   Pages: ◉ All ○ From: [   ] To: [   ]   **Cancel**

Cover Page: ◉ No ○ First Page ○ Last Page

Paper Source: ◉ Paper Cassette ○ Manual Feed

Print: ○ Black & White   ◉ Colour/Greyscale

Destination: ◉ Printer   ○ PostScript® File

Number pages from: [1]

Print: ◉ Records being browsed
        ○ Current record
        ○ Blank record, showing fields [as formatted]   ✓as formatted
        ○ Script: [All scripts]   with boxes
        ○ Field definitions   with underlines

BLANK RECORD

Great option for forms. Fields can become boxes or lines, or be formatted however you choose.

FIELD DEFINITIONS

This prints the information from the *Define Fields* dialog box.
Since some of this info is often cropped in the dialog box, printing it is a good way to see it whole—a VERY USEFUL feature when you're exploring ready-made *templates* (see p. 116).

SCRIPTS

The pop-up menu offers the list of the current file's scripts. You can print one of them, or all of them. Also VERY USEFUL when you explore templates.

63

You can import data from certain types of files into FileMaker Pro. The *Import Records* dialog box shows only files that can be imported from.

You can import data from other FileMaker Pro files, if you wish to add records to your file.

You can import from Excel and other spreadsheets if the data is saved in a standard format. See the list of acronyms below.

Pictures to be imported into a Picture field must also belong to a standard format. Note that you can import Macintosh sounds into a Picture field by pasting.

You can't import from a regular word processor file, however: you must save it first as ASCII ("text only"). The "SomeBooks" file below is a Microsoft Word "text-only" document.

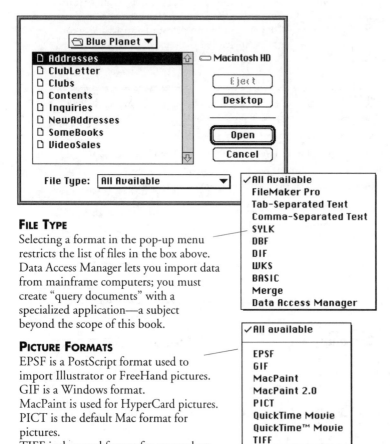

FILE TYPE

Selecting a format in the pop-up menu restricts the list of files in the box above. Data Access Manager lets you import data from mainframe computers; you must create "query documents" with a specialized application—a subject beyond the scope of this book.

PICTURE FORMATS

EPSF is a PostScript format used to import Illustrator or FreeHand pictures.
GIF is a Windows format.
MacPaint is used for HyperCard pictures.
PICT is the default Mac format for pictures.
TIFF is the usual format for scanned art.

MOVIE

When you import a movie into a *Picture* field, Quick-Time controls appear under the field so that you can play the movie. What is imported, actually, is only the first picture of the movie ("Poster") and the address ("path") of the movie file. The rocket won't blast off if the program doesn't find the movie file—e.g., if you've moved it to another folder.

Since the names of books, authors, and publishers all appear in one Microsoft Word document when the reviews are prepared for publication in *Blue Planet* magazine, it is quite easy to put them together as Tab-separated lists—see below. Once imported, the lists become *Books* file records similar to those on p. 43.

Exporting data reverses the process: a document is created in the Text-only (or SYLK, etc.) format, and tab-separated data is exported to it. Note that you can export data to a System 7 *Edition*, to which other programs can *Subscribe*. Whenever you export again, the subscriber's data is updated.

Mindstorms→Seymour Papert→ Basic Books→Harry Kostman¶
A Brief History of Time→ Stephen W. Hawking→ Bantam Books→ Barbara Porter¶
The Mac is not a typewriter→ Robin Williams→ Peachpit Press→ Adam Z. Morbius¶
Why Chimps Can Read→ Ann J. Premack→ Harper & Row→ Helen Fei-shu¶

TAB-SEPARATED LIST

This is what the list looks like in Microsoft Word. The person who typed this list pressed the tab key to separate the future field contents: title–author–publisher–reviewer. The arrows are Word's tab symbols. The Return key marks the separation between two (future) records.

SPECIFY FIELD ORDER

The pointer becomes a double-arrow in the right box. You drag field names up or down to match them with the data in the left box.
Matches are confirmed by clicks in the center band with the checkmark pointer; this changes dotted lines into arrows.
In this example, there is no data for the *Month* field.

SCAN DATA

These buttons let you scan the data to be imported. Clicking the right button would replace *A Brief History of Time* (Record 2) with *The Mac is not a typewriter* (Record 3).

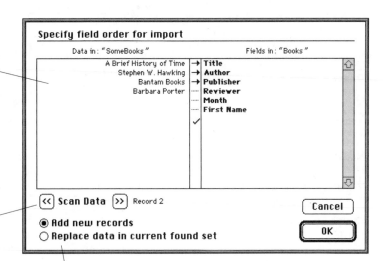

ADD NEW RECORDS

By default, imported data are entered into new records. You can also replace the data of existing records.

The commands in this menu change according to which mode is active: **New Record** becomes **New Layout** or **New Request**. The effect of the commands also change: while in Browse mode you cut, copy, paste, and clear selected data, or select all data inside the active field, in Layout mode you cut, copy, paste, and clear selected objects, or select all objects in the layout.

Clear is not a very useful command: in most cases, you clear selected text or objects by using the Delete key.

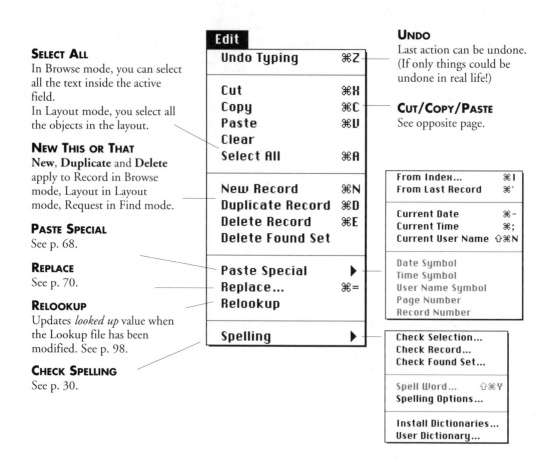

SELECT ALL
In Browse mode, you can select all the text inside the active field.
In Layout mode, you select all the objects in the layout.

NEW THIS OR THAT
New, **Duplicate** and **Delete** apply to Record in Browse mode, Layout in Layout mode, Request in Find mode.

PASTE SPECIAL
See p. 68.

REPLACE
See p. 70.

RELOOKUP
Updates *looked up* value when the Lookup file has been modified. See p. 98.

CHECK SPELLING
See p. 30.

UNDO
Last action can be undone. (If only things could be undone in real life!)

CUT/COPY/PASTE
See opposite page.

Cutting/copying/pasting selected text to/from the Scrapbook or another program, or from one record or file in *Browse* mode to another, is a procedure common to most Macintosh programs.

Cutting/copying/pasting *fields,* however, makes sense only within FileMaker Pro. You can also copy the active record and paste it into a word processing program, where it appears as a tab-separated list.

Graphic objects (including layout text) can be cut/copied/ pasted within FileMaker Pro or to/from other programs. For example, you can buy electronic *clip art* and paste pictures into your layouts.

MOVE TEXT: SELECT AND CUT
Text is selected inside a field by dragging. The **Cut** command is chosen.

Title	Why Chimps Can Read

Author	Premack		
Publisher	Harper & Row	Month	June 1991
Reviewer	Barbara Porter		

CLICK WITH I-BEAM
The insertion point is moved by clicking the I-beam pointer where you want the text to appear.
It can be in the same field, as here, or in another field, another record, another file, or even another program.

Title	Why Chimps Can Read

Author	Premack		
Publisher	Harper & Row	Month	June 1991
Reviewer	Porter,		

PASTE
When the Paste command is chosen, the text appears at the insertion point.
Note that if you paste onto a layout, the text becomes layout text—a Text object.

Title	Why Chimps Can Read

Author	Premack		
Publisher	Harper & Row	Month	June 1991
Reviewer	Porter, Barbara		

COPY A FIELD
If you like the formats of a field (fill, text color, border—see the record number field at right, for example) you can copy it from one layout to another.
If you want to paste it into another file, you should first define a field with the same name and options (here, serial number auto-entry).

Blue Planet: Contents File ?

Subjects	Title	Author	Month
History Portugal Earthquakes Plate Tectonics	The great Lisbon earthquake	Dunod , Harry	June 1993

13

The upper part of the **Paste Special** submenu is available in Browse mode. The commands let you paste special data into the active field.

The lower part of the submenu is available in Layout mode. It lets you paste special Text objects, which appear at the top left corner of the layout and can be moved anywhere.

CURRENT: BROWSE

Current Date and Time are taken from the Mac's clock the moment you paste them, and do not change afterward.

Current User Name is the name that appears in *General Preferences* —see p. 58.

CURRENT: LAYOUT

When you paste the Current Date, Time or User Name in Layout mode, they appear as Text objects, and do not change afterwards.

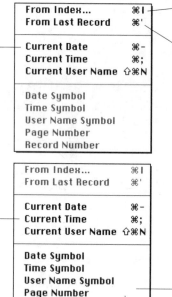

FROM INDEX

See below.

FROM LAST RECORD

See opposite page.

SYMBOLS

In Browse mode, these symbols become the date (updated when you open the file), the time (updated whenever you browse), the User Name (see *Preferences*, p. 58), a question mark and the record number. The ## symbols become the page number in Preview mode and for printing.

INDEX

Selecting a field, then choosing **From Index...** displays the index of words in the selected field for all the records.

You could use the index to review the full list of "subjects," for example, or to check spelling consistency.

Pasting one of these words in Find mode lets you find what records contain this word.

Note that only numbers are indexed in Number fields.

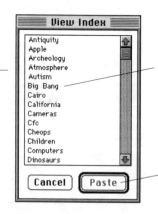

BIG BANG

Big Bang is indexed as one word because Option-Space was typed between Big and Bang. You can index a whole expression in this manner.

PASTE

The index, with its easy-to-remember shortcut (⌘-I), can play the part of a glossary for often-used words.

To import a word, select it and click *Paste,* or simply double-click it.

The "Paste From Last Record" feature, which lets you automate repetitive data entry, is well worth a page because it is a great time saver. Or rather: it is a fantastic time saver if you remember its shortcut: ⌘-'.

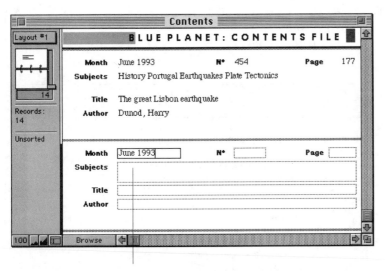

PASTE FROM LAST RECORD

In this example, a new record is created. The *Month* field of the new record is active.

Pressing the ⌘ and ' keys imports the data from the same field in the last active record, i.e. "June 1993."

Pressing ⇧-⌘-' imports the data and also activates the next field. In this case, the next field is N°, where the shortcut would be used again to import "454."

Note that:

1) The data is imported from the last active record—which does not have to be the preceding one.

2) If most fields contain unchanged data, it may be simpler to create the new record with the **Duplicate Record** command, then edit only the fields that must change.

FileMaker Pro's **Replace...** command differs from its counterpart in word processing programs.

Author Victoria Campbell just got married and took her husband's name, Pelegrinelli. You decide to replace Campbell by Pelegrinelli in all the files.

This command replaces the entire contents of a field throughout the found set. It works well here, as you need to search only one field and replace its contents, *Campbell, Victoria,* by *Pelegrinelli, Victoria.*

You can't use this feature to replace a word that appears in several fields, or in the middle of phrases. You may try to export the file to a word processing program, replace the word there, then re-import the file—not a very difficult task in most cases.

FOUND

First step: find records of articles written by Vicky Campbell.
In our small example, there are only two such records.
Second step: write "Pelegrinelli, Victoria" in the author field of one of the records.

Contents

| Layout #1 | **BLUE PLANET: CONTENTS FILE** |

Month: May 1993   N°: 453   Page: 221
Subjects: Atmosphere Pollution South Pole CFC
Title: Can the Ozone Layer be Patched?
Author: Pelegrinelli, Victoria

Records: 14

Found: 2

Unsorted

Month: June 1993   N°: 454   Page: 114
Subjects: Dinosaurs Evolution Fossils Paleontology
Title: But really, why did dinosaurs disappear?
Author: Campbell, Victoria

100 | Browse

REPLACE

When you choose the **Replace...** command, this dialog box appears.
The program checks the active field and the found set of records.
When you click *Replace*, an alert box asks you to confirm the details of the replacement, because you can't undo it.

In the 2 records that you are browsing, permanently replace the contents of the field "Author"?

⦿ Replace with "Pelegrinelli, Victoria "?

◯ Replace with serial numbers

   Initial value: [
   Increment by: [

☐ Update serial number in Entry Options?

[Replace] [Cancel]

The **Replace...** command can be used to "reserialize" (renumber) records.

In the example below, a *Record Number* field was pasted from another file. The Contents file already has 14 records. The auto-entry option will fill this new *Record Number* field when you create new records, but it is not retroactive; thus, the field is empty in the existing records.

Choosing **Replace...** when one of the Record Number fields is active displays the dialog box below.

UPDATE
The Update check box lets you retain the new scheme as Entry Option without having to display the Define Fields and Entry Options

In the 14 records that you are browsing, permanently replace the contents of the field "Record Number"?

○ Replace with ""?

● Replace with serial numbers

   Initial value: [1]

   Increment by: [1]

☐ Update serial number in Entry Options?

[Replace] [Cancel]

SERIAL NUMBERS
Auto-entry serial numbers for new records are defined in the Entry Options dialog box (see p. 44). The numbering scheme for existing records can be changed here. You can serialize a number field that is not auto-numbered; the serial numbers replace whatever it contains.

Contents

Blue Planet: Contents File

Subjects	Title	Author	Month
Egypt Antiquity Archeology Cheops Cairo Ultrasound Pyramids Pharaohs Mummies	The Mystery of the Great Pyramid* Reprinted from The Friends of the British Museum Quarterly	Jacobs, Patricia E.	May 1993
Rockets Relativity Einstein Big Bang Wells Hawkins	Time Travel: Is it Possible?	Morbius, Adam Z.	May 1993
Macintosh Computers Games Software Apple	Best Computer Games on the Macintosh	Grossman, Dmitri	May 1993

Columns

Records: 14

Unsorted

1

2

3

100 Browse

RECORD NUMBER
After the *Replace* button was clicked in the dialog box above, the Record Number fields, which were initially empty, contained these white numbers. The easiest way to number existing records is to paste the @@ symbol onto the layout. Serial numbers inside a field give you more power, because you can edit the numbers, use the field to sort the file, etc.

The **Select** menu is very important. It lets you create fields, switch mode, retrieve data and sort the database.

Beginners often have a hard time with this menu. They go to Layout mode by mistake and don't understand where they are, and how to come back to Browse mode. Also, once they have "found" some records, they forget that the way back to the complete file is through the **Find All** command...

As you are going to use some of the powerful commands in this menu very often, you should learn their keyboard shortcuts as quickly as possible.

MODES
See throughout this book for Browse and Layout, p. 24 for Find, and opposite page for Preview.

REFIND
Takes you back to the last request. See p. 24.

DEFINE FIELDS
See p. 42.

SORT
See p. 28.

VIEW AS LIST
See p. 12.

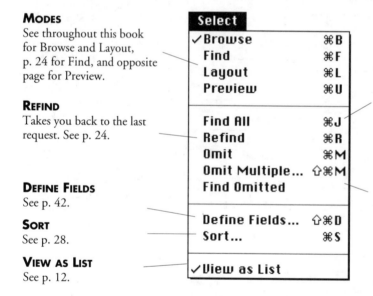

FIND ALL
Takes you back from the found set to the complete file. See p. 23.

OMIT
These commands let you remove the current record from the "found set," or the current record plus a number of records after it (see dialog box below).
You can also omit records by "finding" them (see p. 24). In any case, found set and omitted set are complementary. The **Find Omitted** command switches them.

A special layout of the Book selection is going to be printed. Preview mode is the only way you can see what it is going to look like. For example, the aesthetics of the big page number can't be judged in other modes, since it appears as "##" in Layout mode and "?" in Browse mode.

In this look-but-don't-touch mode, you can't enter data, and most menu commands are dimmed.

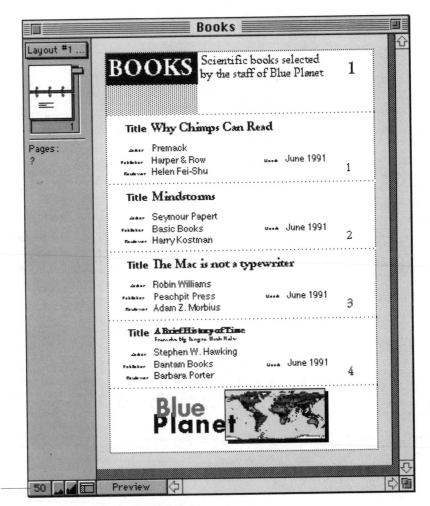

HALF-SIZE
In Preview mode, display your document at 50% size. It's often more convenient— unless you have a large monitor.

The **Layout** and **Arrange** menus are dimmed (with all their commands) when FileMaker Pro is not in Layout mode.

Most of these commands are quite familiar to people who know MacDraw Pro or Illustrator or other graphic programs. Their purpose is to help you resize and position objects, which can be fields, layout text, simple FileMaker Pro designs (lines, rectangles, ovals), or imported pictures.

Rulers, T-Squares, and other designers' tools appear only on the layout. They vanish when you go to another mode.

GRID/RULER LINES
The grid is always invisible, whereas the **Ruler Lines** command lets you show or hide the ruler lines. See opposite page.

SIZE
A palette that gives the location of objects or T-squares. See p. 77.

SHOW
See p. 76.
Sliding and non-printing objects are defined in the **Arrange** menu. See p. 84.

PARTS
See p. 37 and 78.

LAYOUT OPTIONS
Main option is *Columns*. See p. 79.

RULER SETTINGS
Choose unit for rulers and spacing for grid. See opposite page.

RULERS
This command shows or hides the rulers, visible on the opposite page.

T-SQUARES
Akin to what other programs usually call "guides."

SAMPLE DATA
See p. 43 and p. 75.

Layout

Align to Grid	⌘Y
Ruler Lines	
Rulers	
T-Squares	⌘T
Size	
Sample Data	
Show	▶
Define Parts...	
Layout Options...	
Ruler Settings...	

Buttons
Text Boundaries
✓ Field Boundaries
Sliding Objects
Non-Printing Objects
Non-Printable Area

The grid can't be shown below because it is an *invisible* magnetic network that attracts unwary objects when they come close. Working with the grid on is easier, but sometimes less precise than working with the grid off. You can suspend the grid's magnetism by pressing the Command key while you drag.

Ruler lines are visible parallel lines that correspond to markings on the rulers. Ruler Lines in centimeters are tighter than in inches; pixel ruler lines are looser, as they appear only every 100 pixels.

GRID SPACING
Default value for the mesh of the invisible snap-to grid is 6 screen pixels.

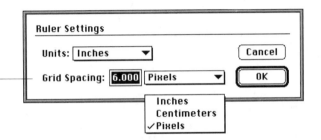

RULER UNIT
The current unit appears in a box at the intersection of the rulers. Clicking this box changes the unit. This is more convenient than changing the unit with the **Ruler Settings...** command, which is useful only for the *Grid Spacing* feature.

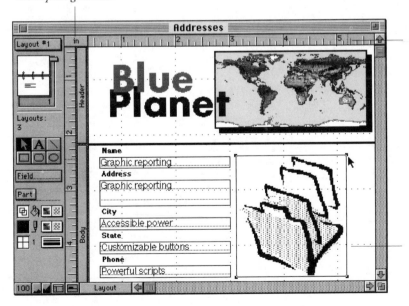

DOTTED
Dotted lines on both rulers show the coordinates of the pointer.

SAMPLE DATA
Sample data let you see what the field will look like in Browse mode. The data is FileMaker Pro propaganda for text fields, and the FileMaker logo for picture fields.

75

MENUS LAYOUT

By default, the fields in Layout mode are marked by a rectangular border ("Field Boundary") which helps to size and position them. See all examples of Layout mode so far. In the picture below, the field boundaries have been hidden, but *Text Boundaries* are shown, as well as the *Non-Printable Area*.

The **Show** submenu lets you show or hide text and field boundaries, and the non-printable area. Buttons, however, as well as sliding and non-printing objects, are always visible. The commands in the submenu let you show special borders (for buttons and non-printing objects) and arrows that mark the sliding direction (for sliding objects—see p. 84).

SHOW SUBMENU
By default, only Field Boundaries are shown.

| Buttons |
| Text Boundaries |
| ✓Field Boundaries |
| Sliding Objects |
| Non-Printing Objects |
| Non-Printable Area |

TEXT BOUNDARIES

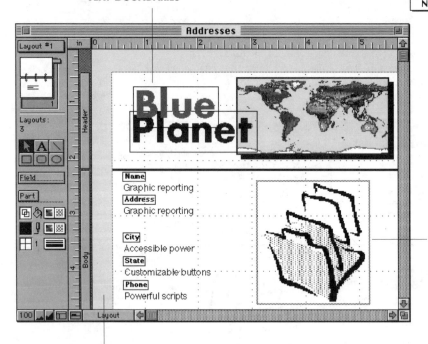

NON-PRINTING
The *Slide Objects* feature (see p. 84) lets you define objects as *Non-Printing*. When you check **Non-Printing Objects** in the **Show** submenu, such objects are marked by a gray border, as here. The command shows or hides the gray border, not the object.

NON-PRINTABLE AREA
When this command is checked, the margins are shown and the origin of the rulers is at the top left corner of the paper sheet.

76

There is one vertical and one horizontal "magnetic" T-square. Although you can use T-squares to position and resize objects with great precision by displaying the Size palette, T-squares are not as versatile as the *guides* found in graphic programs, several of which can be put on the screen at the same time.

OBJECT SIZE

When a rectangular object is selected, the size palette shows the coordinates of its sides, as well as its width and height.

You can position or resize an object by entering numbers into the palette and pressing Return or Enter.

For example, if you want a bitmap picture to look good on a LaserWriter printout, set its width and height to exactly 50% or 75% of its original size (or 48 or 72% if you haven't checked the *Precision Bitmap Alignment* option—see p. 62).

UNIT

Clicking the right side of the palette changes the unit on the palette and on the rulers. Coordinates on the screen can measured exactly in pixels or inches (72 pixels = 1 inch).

They can't, however, be measured exactly in centimeters; you can have 5.997 or 6.032 cm, which is one pixel more, but not 6.000 cm. See example below.

T-SQUARE "SIZE"

When one of the T-squares is moved (notice the double-arrow pointer), the Size palette shows the coordinates of the two T-squares: 5.997-6.032 for the vertical T-square, 6.209-6.244 for the horizontal one.

There are two numbers for each T-square because of their one-pixel (0.035 cm) thickness.

As soon as you stop dragging, the numbers revert to those describing the selected object—or to zero if no object is selected. Thus, you can't edit the coordinates of the T-squares on the palette.

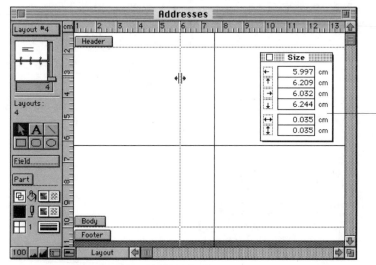

77

There are several ways to add or modify parts. Dragging the *Parts* button from the Status Panel to the layout, or double-clicking the label of an existing part, opens the *Part Definition* dialog box which can be seen on p. 37.

Choosing **Define Parts...** in the **Layout** menu opens the dialog box below; the Part Definition dialog box is then reached through the *Create...* or *Change...* button.

PADLOCK

A double arrow on the left means that the part can move; a padlock means that it can't.

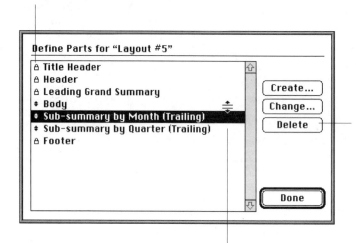

DELETE

The *Delete* button is available only when a part is selected. You can't always delete a selected part. For example, if it contains items, they must be able to migrate to another part. You can delete a Body part if a Header or Footer exists; the Header or Footer then becomes a Title Header or Footer.

SUB-SUMMARY

Headers and footers can never be moved vertically on the page. What you can change is the position of Sub-summary parts relative to each other or to the Body.

For example, the monthly Sub-summary might be dragged above the Body. Its name would then change automatically to *Sub-summary by Month (Leading)*.

The *Layout Options* dialog box is where to rename—or name if you haven't done it at creation time—a layout.

Displaying records in columns is different from "Columnar report," where *fields* are set in columns but records are stacked one under another. It is quite similar to a *Labels* layout.

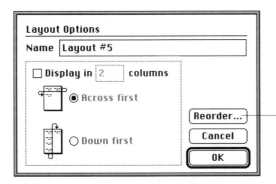

REORDER

The *Reorder...* button lets you display a dialog box with the list of the layouts' names. Drag them up or down to change their order in the Layout pop-up menu at the top of the Status Area.

COLUMNS

This Preview mode picture can be compared to the one on p. 73: obviously, columns let you put more records on the page.

In Layout and Browse mode, records appear one at a time on the left of the screen, like labels. Actually, the Labels layout could be considered a variant of this layout, but without field names. Notice that the order of the records is the default *Across first*.

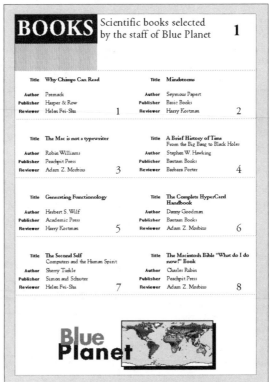

While the **Layout** menu is mostly concerned with the display of objects and their absolute position in the layout, the **Arrange** menu gives you ways of positioning objects relative to each other: align them or move them in front of or behind each other.

The **Slide Objects...** command does not change anything on the screen, but improves layout and aesthetics when the file is printed.

Using the **Tab Order** feature helps you make the file you design more user-friendly.

LOCK

A locked object has gray handles. It can't be moved, changed, cut, or cleared. If it is a text object, as above, it can't be edited. A locked field can't be moved, etc., but its data can be edited normally in Browse mode. A locked object can be copied or grouped. Grouping a locked object with unlocked ones locks the whole group.

Locking objects is a way of protecting them not only against other people's clumsiness, but also against your own.

For example, you might lock a whole layout by choosing the **Select All** and **Lock** commands.

Arrange	
Group	⌘G
Ungroup	⇧⌘G
Lock	⌘H
Unlock	⇧⌘H
Bring to Front	⇧⌥⌘F
Bring Forward	⇧⌘F
Send to Back	⇧⌥⌘J
Send Backward	⇧⌘J
Align Objects	⌘K
Alignment...	⇧⌘K
Slide Objects...	
Tab Order...	

GROUP

See opposite page.

BRING/SEND

Objects belong to planes, or *layers*. An object which is "in front" of another and hides part of it can be sent "behind" it. See p. 82.

ALIGN

This command not only helps you to align objects, but also to "distribute" them evenly. See p. 83.

SLIDE

See p. 84.

TAB ORDER

See p. 85.

Layouts are usually made of bits and pieces: layout texts, fields, FileMaker Pro designs, imported graphics, etc. You often need to move, cut, copy, and paste such objects together. You can select several objects at once, by drawing a selection rectangle with the pointer or by shift-clicking, but you risk leaving one behind. It is much safer to *group* the selected bits and pieces into one object—which you may later *ungroup* if needed.

Among the objects that you are grouping together, one may already be a group. The parts of this object will then be grouped twice; to separate them, you must ungroup twice.

FIVE OBJECTS

Two Text objects; one imported map of the world, its border, and its shadow.
Five objects times four handles equals twenty handles.
With smaller objects, such a proliferation of handles becomes rather messy.

ONE OBJECT

Choosing the **Group** command changes the five selected objects into one object with four handles.
You must **Ungroup** the object if you want to edit the text or change any of the original items.

Objects (including fields and layout text) belong to tracing-paper-like layers.

Bring Forward and **Send Backward** move an object one layer closer or farther; **Bring to Front** and **Send to Back** move an object all the way to the closest or farthest layer. This is a powerful feature of Macintosh graphics programs.

The little game with A, B, and C is quite easy, but may become harder with more objects.

SHADOW
This is what the shadow of the world looked like when it was drawn in front of the picture, before being "sent to back."

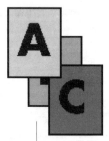

THREE OBJECTS
Each card is made of two grouped objects:
a rectangle and a letter.

BRING FORWARD
A is brought forward one layer. It moves in front of B, but stays behind C.

BRING TO FRONT
Starting from the first picture at left, A is moved all the way to the front.

SEND TO BACK
Starting from the second picture at left, C is moved behind B.

To align objects you must first select them together. FileMaker Pro is willing to align an object with itself, because it is a poor dumb computer program, but you should know better and select at least two objects.

In the dialog box below, "Align top edges" means "align the top edges of objects with the top edge of the topmost object."

It is not possible to distribute the centers of the objects evenly inside their invisible selection rectangle, as in many graphic programs. Instead, what is distributed evenly is the space between the objects, usually quite a different thing.

NONE
If you choose *None* in *Top to Bottom*, objects will not move vertically, but only horizontally.

SAMPLE
The rectangles in the *Sample* box move to show what your choice of alignment looks like.

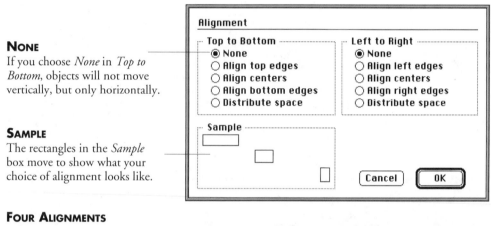

FOUR ALIGNMENTS
A letter and a rectangle have been aligned four different ways: Top-Center (i.e. Top to Bottom: *Align top edges* and Left to Right: *Align centers*), Center-Left, Bottom-Right and Center-Center.

DISTRIBUTE-DISTRIBUTE
Three objects are distributed in a regular way.
As in most graphics programs, you can also "distribute" identical objects with the **Duplicate** command of the **Edit** menu (shortcut: ⌘-**D**).
Select an object, duplicate it and drag the copy where you want it, then duplicate again as many times as you need: the objects are evenly "distributed," because the **Duplicate** command always repeats any custom offset you defined for the first duplication. This feature is called Step-and-Repeat. Try it!
Note that you can also duplicate an object by Option-dragging.

The purpose of the *Slide* feature is to remove excess blank space on labels or in lists.

If a field and an object are selected, and if *Sliding left* is checked in the dialog box below, any blank space at the right of the field will be considered a free zone for the object to slide upon. The object will move as close to the text in the field as possible.

If there are no fields around, the object will not slide.

BLANK SPACE WITHIN
Blank space is removed *within* fields, not *between* fields.

ALL ABOVE
This is checked by default: objects won't go above lowest text among several fields.

ONLY DIRECTLY ABOVE
An object will move up as much as it can, even if it means passing the lowest text among several fields above.

ENCLOSING PART
Size of the enclosing part (e.g., body or footer) might be reduced for records printed as a list, so the next record would move up.
If you are printing labels, do not check this, as labels should have a fixed size.

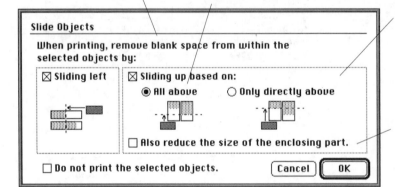

LAYOUT MODE
Sliding Objects has been chosen in the **Show** submenu.
Arrows indicate that *Sliding left* and *Sliding up* have been checked for all the fields.
When first name and surname are separate for sorting purposes, it is necessary to check *Sliding left* for only one field, i. e. First Name.

BROWSE MODE
No sliding. This is how the label would be printed without the *Slide Objects* feature.

PREVIEW MODE
Name and State have slid left; City and State have slid up.
Printed labels and addresses on envelopes obviously look better this way.

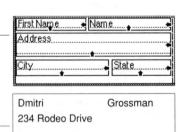

Slide Objects, Tab Order

Although it is possible to move from one field to another by clicking, pressing the Tab key is usually more convenient. The default tab order is: left to right and top to bottom.

In some cases, as in the ad hoc example below, this order is not logical. Instead of entering data into the *Month, Subjects, Title, Author, N°,* and *Page* fields, you would probably prefer *Month, N°, Page, Subjects, Title, Author.*

SEMI-COLUMNS
A compact mixed layout.

		Subjects	Title	Author
Month	May 1991	Macintosh Computers Games Software Apple	Best Computer Games on the Macintosh	Grossman, Dmitri
N°	453			
Page	124			

TAB ORDER
Choosing **Tab Order...** in the **Arrange** menu displays this dialog box, while arrows with numbers showing the tab order sprout on the layout.

EDIT TAB ORDER
Leave the dialog box on screen. If you checked *Edit tab order*, click arrows to edit numbers: type 2 instead of 5, 3 instead of 6, etc. Then click OK in the dialog box.
If you check *Create new tab order*, all the arrows become blank. Just click each field in the order you require, then click OK.
To skip a field, leave its arrow blank.

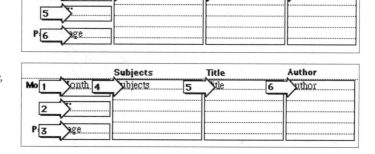

MENUS FORMAT

Format commands are typical of the Macintosh's graphic interface.

In Browse mode, you can change the **Font**, **Size**, **Style** or **Color** of selected text, but all the other commands are dimmed.

In Layout mode, commands apply to selected Text objects or fields. If nothing is selected, commands define the preset format that will be applied to any new Text object or field.

FONT, SIZE
These are standard Macintosh menus controlled by the Macintosh System. In the **Size** submenu, a **Custom...** command lets you choose a size from 1 to 500 pt.

TEXT COLOR
The **Color** submenu is shown on p. 47.

TEXT FORMAT
This command is available for any kind of field. See opposite page.

PICTURE FORMAT
See p. 31.

FIELD BORDERS
See p 91.

CASE
In an *UPPERCASE* field, data is uppercase even when you type lowercase.
In a *lowercase* field, data is lowercase even when you type uppercase.
Title Case means: first letter uppercase, then lowercase.
For a default field, none of these commands is checked—you define case with the Shift key.

ALIGN TEXT
Full justification does not look good for narrow fields because FileMaker Pro does not hyphenate words.

LINE SPACING
The number you set in **Custom...** (from -127 pt to 127 pt) is displayed at the bottom of the menu, for example "2 Point."

NUMBER, DATE, TIME
See pp. 88 and 89.

FIELD FORMAT
See p. 90.

STYLE
These commands "toggle": you choose **Bold** either to make selected text bold or not bold.

SUPERSCRIPT, SUBSCRIPT
These commands raise or lower text and make it smaller.
You would use them in Browse mode for selected text, e.g. for exponents, rather than in Layout mode for entire fields.

Text Format

When you want to change the format of a few words in Browse mode, it's easy to do so in the **Style** submenu.

However, if you need to set all the attributes of fields in a layout, going to all the submenus is a waste of time. It is simpler to use the *Text Format* dialog box; a sample sentence shows you what the text will look like with the attributes you have chosen.

SELECTION
The "Subjects" field was selected in Layout mode, and the **Text Format...** command was chosen.

NO SELECTION
When no Text object or field has been selected, the dialog box says *Default Text Format.* Attributes will apply to all new fields or Text objects.
As for other object and field formats, default Text formats can be defined *by imitation:* just Command-click a field or Text object to make all its formats the default ones.

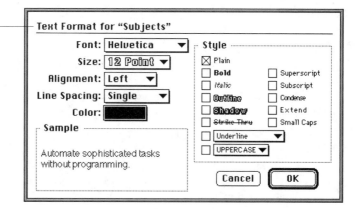

SAMPLE
The Sample box shows 18 pt Futura Bold white text, Small Caps, Centered, with -4 pt custom line spacing.
Note that a FileMaker Pro text with 18 pt size and -4 pt line spacing is what other programs call a text with 18 pt size and 14 pt line spacing (or "leading").

87

As with text format, you can define a *Default Number Format* and decimal options for new number fields—either in the dialog boxes below or *by example* when you Command-click a field.

You can also choose a number format and decimal options for selected number fields: for example, you can put some fields with currency symbols and some without in the same record.

The preset number format and options may change according to the versions of the Macintosh system and of FileMaker Pro you are using. In France, the sample number below would be written -6 543,9871.

FORMATTED AS ENTERED

This button is checked by default when you open a new file.

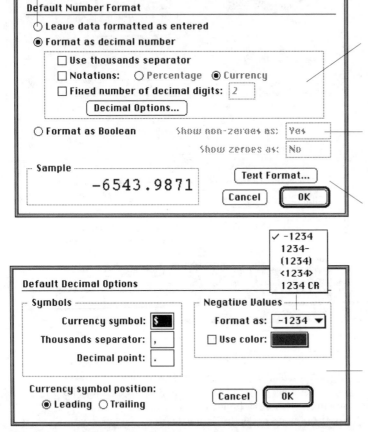

FIXED NUMBER

With 2 decimal digits, the sample number is rounded to −6543.99; number 5 becomes 5.00.

With −2 decimal digits, 425 is rounded to 400.

The unrounded number is retained for calculations.

BOOLEAN

A calculation field could include a formula like **Profit>Debt** (where *Profit* and *Debt* are field names). The result is 1 if true, 0 if false. *Format as Boolean* will replace 1 with Yes and 0 with No.

TEXT FORMAT

This button opens the *Text Format* dialog box.

The text format of the number was set to Courier 24, aligned right, as can be seen in the Sample box.

DECIMAL OPTIONS

This dialog box appears when you click the *Decimal Options...* button above.

Example of a *Leading* currency symbol: $45.

Trailing currency symbol: 45 F.

The **Date Format** defines how a "//" layout date object or a field date is displayed. It applies either to selected layout date objects or fields or, when nothing is selected, to new layout dates or fields. Note that for a date field, the date must be *entered* in a standard format like 10/31/91, which depends on the national settings of your system.

The **Time Format...** command opens a dialog box similar to the main one below.

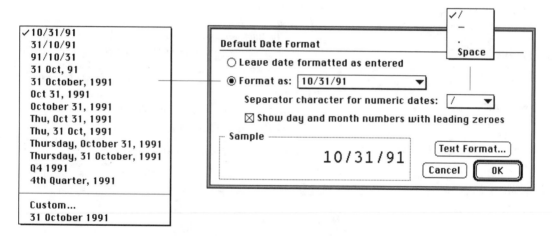

Custom

Choosing **Custom...** in the pop-up menu displays the dialog box below: seven pop-up menus let you define elements and separators for the date. In our example, a date entered in the field as 10/31/91 is displayed as Oct 91 as soon as you click outside the field or press Enter.

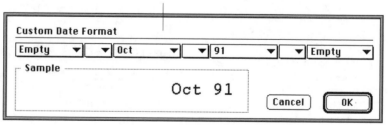

You don't need the *Field Format* feature if you only include plain fields in your layouts. It lets you add a scroll bar to fields and make choices for fields with value lists and repeating fields.

Here, a *Repeating field* was selected before the **Field Format...** command was chosen. You can also define Preset formats when no field is selected, or format by imitation.

Repeating, Calculation, and Summary fields, which are easy to use but may be tricky to create, are explained in examples from p. 100 on.

SCROLL BAR
Including a vertical scroll bar is a must for overflowing read-only fields.

VALUE LIST
See p. 35. You can add an **Other...** item to create an "open" value list.

REPETITIONS
A repeating field looks like any other field until you decide how many repetitions will be shown. Default orientation is vertical. See a vertical example on p. 100; see a horizontal example below.

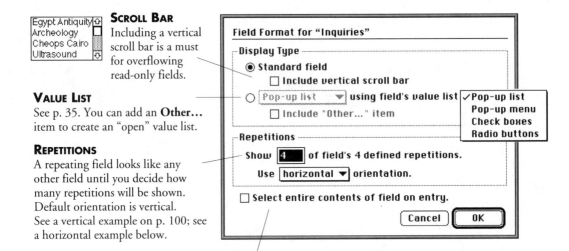

ENTIRE CONTENTS
Check this if field's data is usually to be replaced rather than edited.

REPEATING FIELD
Blue Planet's librarian counts the number of telephone inquiries for each article, with a breakdown in four categories.
Three horizontal records are displayed in this example.
Numbers like 18, 44, 26, and 57 (in the first record) all belong to one number field, called *Inquiries*, defined as Repeating in the *Options* dialog box (see p. 44).
Horizontal orientation is chosen for the Inquiries field in the *Field Format* dialog box above.

TOTAL
You don't enter anything in *Total* fields, which contain a formula, "Sum (Inquiries)," and are filled by the program.
Total for year, in a Trailing Grand Summary part, displays the total for all browsed records, here January to May.

BLUE PLANET	Inquiries about Articles					
Month	Article	Children	Teens	Adults	Schools	Total
5	Mystery Great Pyramid	18	44	26	57	145
5	Time Travel: Possible?	40	65	20	33	158
5	Best Games Macintosh	52	351	35	8	446
					Total for year	1671

Field Format, Borders

The word "Borders" in **Field Borders...** doesn't tell the whole story: this command also lets you choose a fill for the selected field or fields. When no field is selected (first example below), default borders and fill apply to new fields.

For inverted text (second example below), you must choose a dark fill for the field or Text object and a light color for the text.

BORDERS

A field has four "borders."
Note that when a field has a scroll bar (see opposite page), it appears only when the field is active. If you want it to be permanently visible, give the field a right border.

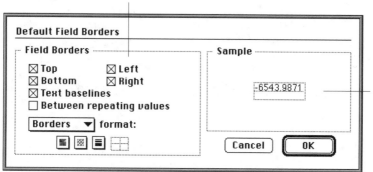

BASELINES

This sample has a *baseline.*
You may use baselines in any field for aesthetic reasons, but they are especially useful in forms.

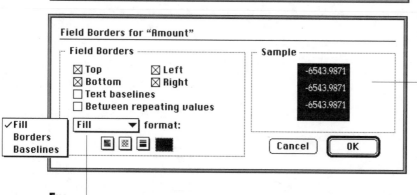

REPEATING

The sample reflects the fact that *Amount* is a repeating field. A repeating field may have "borders" between the repetitions.

FILL

You can choose one format for borders (here: 2 pt black line), another for baselines, and yet another for fill.
When the sample looks good, click OK to apply your choice.
Note that you can also choose a fill in the Status Area.

A FileMaker Pro *script* tells the computer to execute a series of user-defined actions. To create a script, you can either choose "steps" in a list, or show and tell the program what actions to remember and perform.

If you go the show-and-tell route, you must perform the actions to be automated *before* choosing **ScriptMaker....** The command displays the dialog box below, which lets you name the script. Then you check the steps of the script in a second dialog box, shown on the opposite page.

SCRIPTMAKER
Displays the dialog box below, which shows the full list of all the scripts and lets you name a new script.

LIST OF SCRIPTS
The dialog box below lets you decide whether script names appear here.

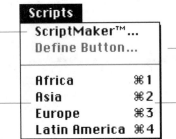

DEFINE BUTTON
This command is available only when an object is selected in Layout mode. See p. 94.

SHORTCUTS
There is no limit to the number of scripts you can create, but the menu will display only fifty. The first ten are given keyboard shortcuts.

LATIN AMERICA
These scripts belong to the example on p. 108. Dragging names up or down here changes their order of appearance in the menu.

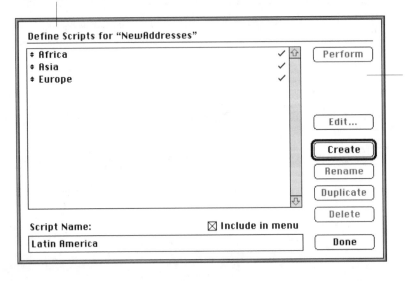

DEFINE SCRIPTS
All the scripts for the current file are listed here.
If you want to display a name in the menu, select it and check the *Include in menu* box. An empty script named "-" (a hyphen) becomes a separating line in the menu. The *Edit...* and *Create...* buttons lead to the *Script Definition* dialog box shown on the opposite page.

The dialog box below offers a list of all the possible steps in a script, at left, and a tentative script describing the actions you just performed, at right. Options let you fine-tune the script. You can also build a new script (if you haven't performed any action) by selecting available steps and moving them to the right box.

These two pages only show the skeleton of the script-making process. See p. 108 for a complete, yet simple, example.

AVAILABLE STEPS

There are more than sixty possible steps—see a complete list on p. 112. When you select a step, the *Clear* button becomes *Move*, so that you can add it to the step list on the right. You can also double-click a step to select it. Notice that the first available step is *Perform Script [...]*. This lets you nest *sub-scripts* inside scripts to automate complex processes. See p. 112.

STEP LIST

This list usually adds some common steps, like *Sort* and *Print*, to the steps you just performed. They were deleted here.

OPTIONS

The *Options* box changes according to the type of step selected in the list. It can contain check boxes, pop-up menus, and buttons that display dialog boxes.

It often includes a *Pause* option, similar to the *Pause/Resume Script* step, which lets the user enter data, etc.

When the script is paused, a *Continue* button appears in the Status Area (see picture below). Clicking this button resumes the script.

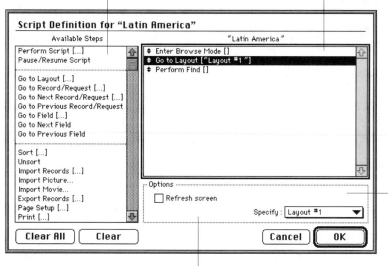

SPECIFY, REFRESH

Once *Go to Layout ["Layout #1"]* has been selected, relevant options appear in the *Options* box. Here, a pop-up menu shows the list of existing layouts in the file. Choosing a layout changes the step's bracketed argument.

A script is usually performed as fast as possible, without any refreshing of the screen. If you want the user to follow what's happening, you can ask the program to refresh the screen after a step—but you can't keep the step list on screen, as you can in HyperCard and other programs when "debugging."

MENUS SCRIPTS

A Macintosh button is a sensitive part of the screen: something happens when you click it.

The **Define Button...** command is usually dimmed. To highlight it, you must go to Layout mode and select an object, or several objects of any kind except *field*. Each selected object becomes a button. Clicking it in Browse mode then performs a script or any action you choose in the list.

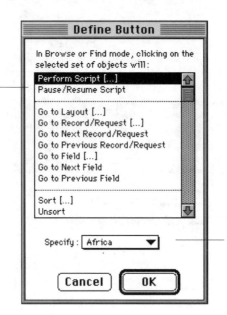

AVAILABLE STEPS
This list is similar to the list in the *Script Definition* dialog box— see p. 112.
If you want a click on the button to perform one step, just select it here.
If you want a click to perform several steps, create a script with these steps and name it, then select *Perform Script [...]* here.

SPECIFY
Options appear here when you select a step with [...] brackets. For example, when you choose the *Perform Script [...]* step, a pop-up menu lists the file's scripts.
In other cases, options can include check boxes, buttons leading to dialog boxes, etc. FileMaker Pro's User Guide gives a full list of options.

BUTTONS TEMPLATE
These buttons belong to the Contents screen of the *Buttons Template*.
Clicking one of them displays button samples. See opposite page.
Note the difference between the inverted *Menu* button, and the plain version on the opposite page.

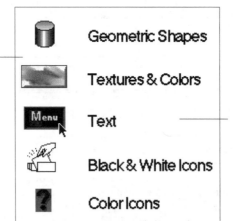

INVERTED
When an object becomes a button, it behaves like a standard Macintosh button: when you move the pointer over the object and press down the button of the mouse, the object is inverted.
If you release the mouse button while the object is inverted, the step or script is performed.
If you move the pointer out of the object, it ceases to be inverted and nothing happens when you release the mouse button.

94

Any object can become a button (see examples on p. 110), but most Macintosh users have certain expectations about a button's look.

One way you can help users identify your buttons quickly is to import some of the pictures below from FileMaker Pro's *Buttons* template. Note that the pictures with names are effective buttons—with scripts attached.

The HyperCard Developers' Kit also offers nice buttons, but in black and white only.

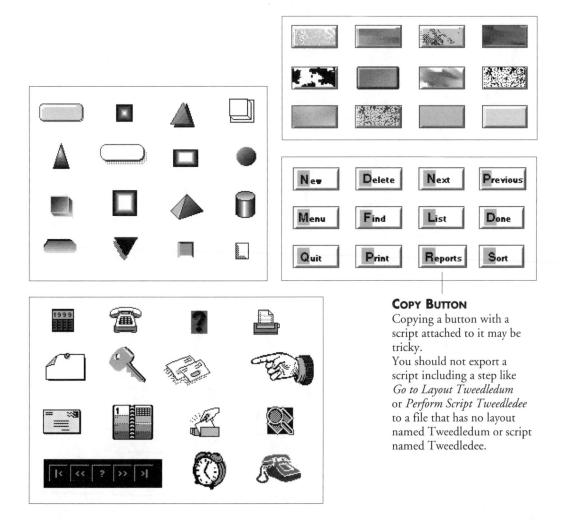

COPY BUTTON

Copying a button with a script attached to it may be tricky.

You should not export a script including a step like *Go to Layout Tweedledum* or *Perform Script Tweedledee* to a file that has no layout named Tweedledum or script named Tweedledee.

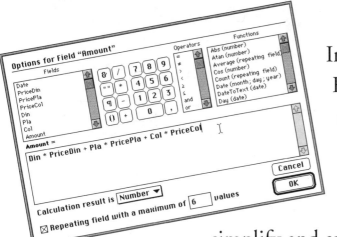

In this section, FileMaker Pro's advanced features are explained through examples. These features let you simplify and automate tasks so that the files become much easier to use.

The designer may have to invest some time to understand the advanced features and to implement them, but this investment is repaid a hundredfold in time saved by the users.

Blue Planet science clubs exist in several cities. When a reader wants to know the address of a club in his or her city, the librarian opens a file called *ClubLetter* and enters the name of the city into a new record. The program then "looks up" a file called *Clubs* and imports the address of the club into the letter.

February 7, 1994

Dear Reader,

    Thank you for your letter. Yes, there is a Blue Planet Club in

Its address is

BLANK LETTER

This is a new record of the *ClubLetter* file, seen in Browse mode. The Tab key was pressed so that the outlines of the fields are visible.
Text outside the fields is Layout Text, which appears on all records.

WINDOW MENU

When you enter the name of a city after the word *in*, the program opens the *Clubs* address file but hides it.
The names of hidden windows appear inside parentheses in the **Window** menu. You can open a hidden window by choosing its name in the menu. You can hide any window.

Window
Hide Window

✓ **ClubLetter**
Contents
(Clubs)

Ruth Mortensen
17, Copperfield Place
Chicago Ill 60614

February 7, 1994

Dear Reader,

    Thank you for your letter. Yes, there is a Blue Planet Club in Chicago.
Its address is 214 North Clark St #702 (312) 427 4550.

FINISHED LETTER

As soon as you write "Chicago," the program looks up in the *Clubs* file and imports data about the city's Blue Planet Club into the *Address* and *Phone* fields.
This is what the letter looks like—in Preview mode.
Notice that the Text object periods (barely visible in Browse and Layout modes) have slid nicely behind Chicago and the phone number.
The **Relookup** command (see p. 66) lets you update a file like this one when the lookup file has changed.

Now, see how it's done. In this example, the whole process would have to be repeated for the *Phone* field.

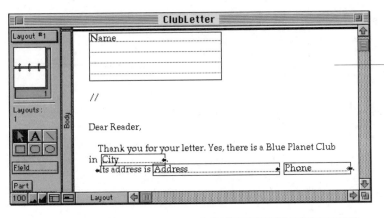

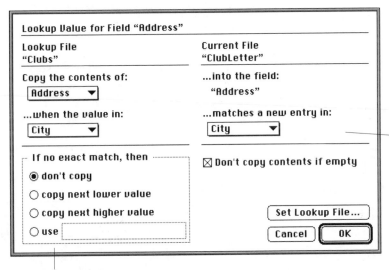

CURRENT FILE
To begin the Lookup process, choose **Define Fields...** in the **Select** menu (see p. 42).
Select the field into which lookup data will appear automatically (here, the *Address* field) in the Define fields dialog box, and click the *Options...* button.

ENTRY OPTIONS
This is the bottom of the Options dialog box (see the whole dialog box on p. 44).
Check *Look up values from a file* and click *Set Lookup....* An Open-type dialog box lets you choose the Lookup file—here, *Clubs*. Then the dialog box at left appears.

LOOKUP VALUES
Pop-up menus with names of the current and Lookup files' fields let you choose where to look up the data.
Note that:
1) While values inside fields must match, field names can be different; it is easier to work with matching field names, however.
2) Keeping the Lookup file and active file inside the same folder speeds up the Lookup process.

NO EXACT MATCH
When there is *no exact match*, the program is willing to look up the next value. This makes sense for a range of numbers, but you can also apply this feature to text. For example, with a slightly reworded letter, you could send a Cleveland reader to Chicago.
You can also use a brief (254-character) excuse, e.g. "Sorry, no Blue Planet Club in your city!"

99

A *repeating field* is a very convenient device for tables (see opposite page): instead of duplicating a field and grouping the duplicates, you have only one object, which you can move and format easily.

Its main purpose, however, is to let you do wonders with the *Functions* that take repeating fields as arguments: *Average, Max, StDev, Sum,* etc. See examples in the following pages—and a complete list of functions on p. 126.

ENTRY OPTIONS DIALOG BOX

Here again is the bottom of the Entry Options dialog box (shown on p. 44), where fields are defined as "repeating." The six-values field mentioned here belongs to the example on the opposite page.

> ☐ Prohibit modification of auto-entered values
> ☒ Repeating field with a maximum of [6] values
> ☐ Use a pre-defined value list: [Edit Values...]
> ☐ Look up values from a file: [Set Lookup...]

FIELD FORMAT DIALOG BOX

In the Field Format dialog box (see p. 90), you decide the number of repetitions to be shown.
Here, the orientation is vertical.

> ┌ Repetitions ─────────────────────
> │ Show [6] of field's 6 defined repetitions.
> │ Use [vertical ▼] orientation.

REPEATING TEXT FIELD

While repeating fields usually contain numbers, there is no law against a repeating Text field like this one.
Repetitions act like different fields when you tab (don't press Return), but like one field when you create a *Find* request.
Only the first repetition is considered when you sort.

HANDLES

Whatever the number of repetitions, the handles keep to the corners of the first one.

> Name

LOOKUP

In this international variant of p. 98's Lookup example, the field which was called *City* is now a Calculation field with the formula: "Last(Name)".
This means that the last line of the *Name* repeating field—the country—is entered automatically into this field. Notice that it doesn't have a dotted border anymore, because you can't write in it.
The rest of the Lookup process is as before. Oh, don't worry about the period to the right of France: it will slide in due time.

> Marie Claire Dunod
> 11 bis rue Boissy d'Anglas
> 75008 Paris
> France
>
> 15/12/93
>
> Dear Reader,
>
> Thank you for your letter. Yes, there is a Blue Planet Club in France.
> Its address is 22 rue Beautreillis 75004 Paris (1) 48 87 28 27

The default field in FileMaker Pro is a text field. Thus, the examples in this book have been built mostly around words. However, FileMaker Pro is great for numbers, too.

Blue Planet's librarian sells Blue Planet videotapes, and keeps track of weekly sales with the file below.

You don't need to know anything about repeating fields to use such a file; you just enter the data line after line.

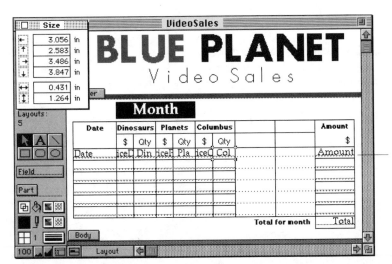

VERTICAL
The eight columns with data are vertical repeating fields—all number fields except the first one: *Date, PriceDin* (under the first $ sign), *Din, PricePla, Pla, PriceCol, Col* and *Amount.* Din is short for dinosaurs, Pla for Planets, Col for Colombus.
The boxes and dotted lines are layout designs.
Notice the Size palette: it is useful when you want to create fields of the same size.

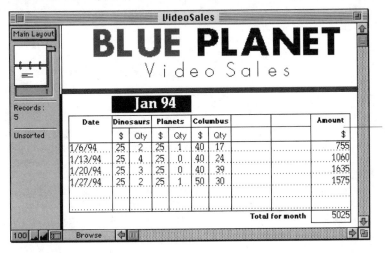

CALCULATION
Amount and *Total* are Calculation fields; numbers appear or change automatically as soon as you modify data inside the *$* or *Qty* fields.
The formula for *Total* uses *Amount* as argument (see p. 103).
The *Qty* fields are also summed automatically, but the totals are not visible here. See p. 104.

101

When you define a field as "Calculation" in the *Define Fields* dialog box, the *Create* button displays the dialog box below.

You must then indicate a calculation formula for the field. This formula often involves other fields as arguments.

In Browse mode, the formula is computed when you enter data into the argument fields, so that the result is displayed automatically inside the Calculation field when you leave an argument field.

A Calculation field is *read-only*. You can select it (by clicking or pressing the tab key) and copy it, and scroll it if it has a scroll bar, but you can't edit it.

TEXT OPERATORS
& lets you fuse two text strings into one.
" " tells the program that the text inside is a constant rather than a field name. Return sign ("¶") moves to the next line.

MATH OPERATORS
Usual mathematical precedence order can be changed by using parentheses.

OPERATORS
Boolean operators. An expression like **Din<Pla** (meaning that the value of the Pla field is bigger than the value of the Din field) returns True or False.

FUNCTIONS
See full list on p. 126.

FIELDS
This box contains the full list of existing fields.

FORMULA
Field and function names, operators, and numbers can be entered by double-clicking or by typing from the keyboard. This box can contain up to 32,000 characters, but if you really want to create a very long formula, you may find it easier to type it inside some text field, then copy and paste it here.

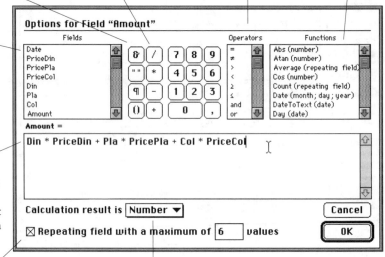

REPEATING
You can define a *Calculation* field as repeating here or in the Entry Options dialog box.

RESULT
You could choose to define a number or date as text. Sorting order is different when months are considered alphabetically rather than chronologically. Numbers are found whole; for example, considering phone numbers as text lets you find numbers beginning with "212."

The layout shown on p. 101 has been expanded below, so that the names of the fields are readable.

The repeating Calculation field for *Amount* uses several repeating number fields—which are filled by the librarian—as arguments.

The *Total* Calculation field has the *Amount* field as argument.

Three hidden fields are shown here; they are similar to the *Total* field but are designed for another layout, which you can see ion the following page.

PRICEDIN*DIN + PRICEPLA*PLA + PRICECOL*COL

This is the formula for the *Amount* field. In repeating fields, the formula applies to each repetition:

Line 1 of Amount = (Line 1 of PriceDin) * (Line 1 of Din) + etc.
Line 2 of Amount = (Line 2 of PriceDin) * (Line 2 of Din) + etc.

Make sure you don't skip a line by mistake in one of the fields.

When any number is changed, e.g. when the price of the very successful *Columbus* video is raised from $40 to $50, the formula is re-computed instantly and the numbers in *Amount* and *Total* change right away.

Month							
Date	**Dinosaurs**		**Planets**		**Columbus**		**Amount**
	$	Qty	$	Qty	$	Qty	$
Date	PriceDin	Din	PricePla	Pla	PriceCol	Col	Amount
	QtyDin		QtyPla		QtyCol		
					Total for month		Total

SUM(AMOUNT)

This is the formula for the *Total* Calculation field.
The *Sum* function takes the name of a repeating field as argument, and sums its contents.

SUM(DIN)

This is the formula attributed to the *QtyDin* field when it was created in the *Define Fields* dialog box.

This Calculation field, which sums the quantity of Dinosaurs videos sold each month, is shown with a dotted border for demonstration purpose, but in fact it is hidden in this layout. Same thing for *QtyPla* and *QtyCol*. More about this on p. 104.

ADVANCED

In the Main Layout of the *VideoSales* file, shown on pp. 101 and 103, a record contains repeating fields for one month of sales. The number of videotapes sold each month is totalled in hidden fields called *QtyDin, QtyPla,* and *QtyCol,* shown on p. 103.

The Layout below takes up these fields to build one-line monthly records.

A Sub-Summary part (see how to create one on p. 37) houses Summary fields. Such fields do not handle data belonging to a repeating field or to several fields in a record, like the function **sum** of a Calculation field, but the data in *one* field throughout several records.

ONE MORE FIELD

A *Quarter* field was added, because the summing up in the Sub-Summary part is done quarterly.

Even though the records are ordered chronologically, a *Sort by Quarter* has to be performed for the Sub-Summary part to be displayed; the sort field is chosen when the Sub-Summary part is created (see p. 37).

	Month	Dinosaurs	Planets	Columbus	Total
1	Jan 94	11	2	110	123
1	Feb 94	5	2	176	183
1	Mar 94	7	5	252	264
Average for Quarter		7.7	3.0	179.3	190.0
2	Apr 94	5	2	208	215
2	May 94	9	7	187	203
Average for Quarter		7.0	4.5	197.5	209.0
Average for Year		7.4	3.6	186.6	197.6

SUB-SUMMARY

After three records belonging to the same quarter (or fewer when the quarter is not over), the average quantity of videotapes sold appears in a Sub-Summary part.

Below the last record, a Trailing Grand Summary part shows the average for the year so far.

A default Summary field would show the total quantity sold, not the average.

You change this in the Summary Options dialog box.

See opposite page.

PREVIEW

Sub-Summary parts are not displayed in Browse mode, but only in Preview mode.

104

What a Summary field summarizes depends on its position in the Layout. As can be seen on the opposite page and below, putting the same Summary field in a *Sub-Summary* part and in a *Trailing Grand Summary* part does not yield the same result.

NUMBER FIELDS
The numbers in the Calculation fields (*QtyDin*, etc.) are entered automatically by the program, but they could be entered by the user if the field wasn't a Calculation field. It doesn't matter: as long as there are numbers in the fields, they can be summarized.

FORMULA FOR A QUARTER
You could enter 1, 2, 3 or 4 into the *Quarter* field, but it is also possible to make this a Calculation field. Can you devise a formula?
See a possible answer on p. 127.

SUB-SUMMARY
Sub-Summary part, Summary fields.

TRAILING GRAND SUMMARY
This part houses the same fields as the Sub-Summary part, but instead of displaying quarterly summaries, they'll show summaries for the whole file.

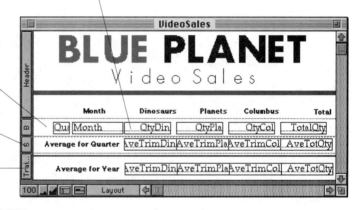

SUMMARY OPTIONS
When the field is defined as "Summary" in the *Define Fields* dialog box, clicking the Create button displays this dialog box, which replaces *Entry Options*.

TOTAL
The default command in this pop-up menu is **Total**.
Some commands come with options: you can have a *Running Total* and *Running Count*, weigh an average (e.g., weigh cost by quantity), and subtotal a *Fraction of Total* after sorting in the same way you sub-summarize.

FIELDS
This pop-up menu shows the names of all the fields in the file, including hidden ones.

ADVANCED

FileMaker Pro's network feature lets Adam Z. Morbius consult the *Contents* file on the Macintosh of the librarian (named Margaret Barski for this example) if:

1. His ("Guest") and her ("Host") computers belong to the same network—AppleTalk (Macintosh) or mixed.

2. The *Contents* file is open on her computer.

3. She has un-checked the **Single-User** command in the **File** menu of *Contents*.

4. FileMaker Pro for Macintosh or Windows is installed and open on his computer.

5. His FileMaker Pro is not a copy of hers.

6. He remembers his password.

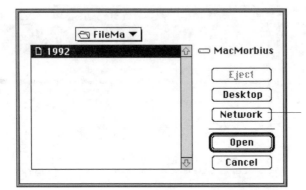

NETWORK

Morbius opens the FileMaker Pro application or a FileMaker Pro document on his computer, then chooses the **Open...** command in the **File** menu.

Clicking the *Network* button displays the dialog box below. The shortcut ⌥-⌘-**O** takes you directly to the dialog box below, without displaying this one.

ACCESS

The box is empty if no multi-user FileMaker Pro file is open on the network.

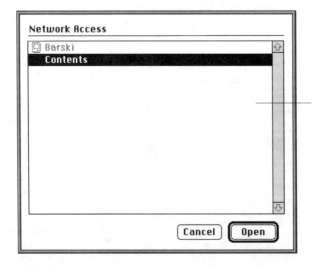

Any Macintosh or PC with an open FileMaker Pro multi-user file appears here, provided the host's FileMaker Pro is not a copy of the guest's (in which case the program would not run at all).

The System 7 file-sharing feature also lets you consult a file on a distant Macintosh —but the file must be closed, not open as it is here. If the file is installed on an AppleShare server, the first person to open it can become host to others.

When Morbius tries to open a protected file like *Contents*, he is asked for the password and must answer Newton, Einstein or Curie. What he can do with the file depends on the password he uses (i.e., which group he belongs to; see p. 60).

With the FileMaker Pro network function, a guest may not define fields, import/export data, change access privileges or save a copy (note that the System 7 file-sharing feature places no such restriction on the guest). When the host wishes to perform one of these exclusive tasks, or to close the file on his or her computer, the program first asks the guests to close the file. See below.

CAN'T CLOSE
If Margaret Barski tries to close *Contents* while Morbius is consulting the file, this dialog box is displayed on her screen.

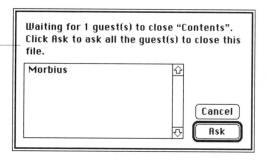

MESSAGE
When Margaret Barski clicks the *Ask* button, Morbius sees this polite message on his screen.

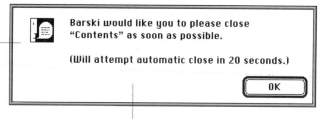

MORE ABOUT NETWORK POLITENESS

When a guest activates a field, it is effectively locked to other guests. As a guest, don't go to lunch without closing the file. This is especially true when there are many guests: maximum number is twenty-five, but a certain sluggishness sets in at twelve guests or so.

As a host, don't forget to open the files that people might want to share (you can use the **Hide Window** command if you don't need to consult these files yourself)—including all the files involved in *Lookups*—and to make them Multi-User.

In a cross-platform setup, avoid strange fonts, special characters, Outline and Shadow styles, QuickTime, Apple Events in scripts, and so forth.

ADVANCED

Blue Planet keeps a special international address file (called *NewAddresses*) for science resources like universities, publishers and companies.

Non-U.S. addresses are divided into four zones: Africa, Asia-Australia, Europe, and Latin America.

The simple example on these two pages shows how the process of finding the addresses within a zone was automated.

Other scripts can be studied in the *Templates* and *Apple Events Examples* files supplied with FileMaker Pro (see p. 116).

ZONE FIELD

The layout of this file includes a *Zone* field, which could be filled by clicking one of four zone names in a value list.

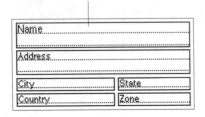

CREATING THE EUROPE SCRIPT (1)

1) **Find** is chosen in the **Select** menu.
2) *Europe* is entered into the Zone field.
3) The *Find* button is clicked.

CREATING THE EUROPE SCRIPT (2)

4) The Layout is switched from *Layout #1* to *Resources*.
5) Preview mode is chosen.

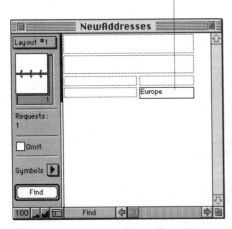

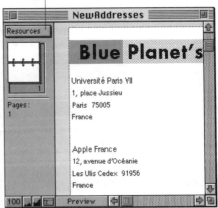

Script Example

Choosing **ScriptMaker...** in the **Scripts** menu after performing the actions described at the bottom of the opposite page displays the dialog box shown on p. 92. After naming your new script, another dialog box appears (shown on p. 93), which contains a ready-made "Step List" inspired by the just-performed actions. You may need to improve the Step list—see below.

The complete sequence should be repeated for each continent.

CREATING THE EUROPE SCRIPT (3)

When this script was created, the program changed the order of the *Find* and *Go to Layout* steps; there is no harm in this. The *Enter Preview Mode* step was missing altogether. You must check the steps listed by the program very carefully. A double-click on *Enter Preview Mode [...]* in the list of Available Steps added it to the list below.

The Script is now ready. It can be performed either by selecting it in the *Define Scripts* dialog box and clicking *Perform,* or by choosing it at the bottom of the **Scripts** menu. As neither of these methods is convenient, it will be attached to a button. See next page.

RESTORE

"Perform Find [Restore]" means: Restore the Find Request to what it was when the script was created—i.e., Zone=Europe. To see explicit arguments of a script (i.e., actual Find requests like Zone=Europe, as well as actual Page setups, Sort orders, Import/Export orders) instead of the word *Restore,* print the script.

```
⇕ Go to Layout ["Resources"]
⇕ Perform Find [Restore]
⇕ Enter Preview Mode [Pause]
```

EDIT A SCRIPT

Suppose that now you want to modify a script.
Perform new steps (say, Find Eurasia instead of Europe), then choose **ScriptMaker...**, select the script's name, and click *Edit....* This dialog box gives you a choice: do you want to keep or replace the arguments? That is, restore to the new improved Find request (Eurasia), or keep the former one (Europe)?

The following information is needed to perform this script. You can:

- **Keep the information already saved for this script**
- **Replace it with the information currently in use**

	Keep	Replace
Page Setup:	○ Keep	○ Replace
Import Order:	○ Keep	○ Replace
Find Requests:	◉ Keep	○ Replace
Sort Order:	○ Keep	○ Replace
Export Order:	○ Keep	○ Replace

Cancel   OK

ADVANCED

The words "Africa," "Europe," etc., have been written as Text objects and defined as buttons. Each button calls up the script bearing its name. You could also put transparent buttons over the continents themselves.

FROM OBJECT TO BUTTON
The Text object *Europe* is given a color so that the user can identify it more easily as a button.
It is selected and the **Define Button...** command is chosen.

FROM SCRIPT TO BUTTON
This dialog box lets you select an existing script for the button.
You can test the script, and change it, before or after you attribute it to the button.

Button Example

When the *Europe* button is clicked in Browse mode, the
Layout is changed to *Resources;* then Europe addresses are found
and shown in Preview mode (notice that fields have slid left).

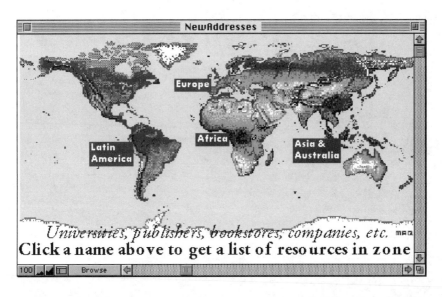

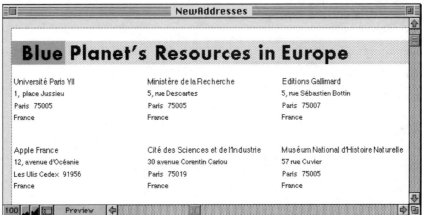

ADVANCED

The complete list of available steps for scripts is given below. While most of these steps are straightforward and easy to understand, two of them can lead to complex developments: *Perform Script [...]*, which lets you nest *Sub-scripts* inside the script (see below), and *Send Apple Event [...]*, which makes it possible to command other applications.

STEPS: A COMPLETE LIST

Perform Script [...]	Omit	Paste [...]
Pause/Resume Script	Omit Multiple [...]	Clear [...]
Go to Layout [...]	Find Omitted	Select All
Go to Record/Request [...]	Enter Browse Mode [...]	Spell Check Selection [...]
Go to Next Record/Request	Enter Find Mode [...]	Spell Check Record
—Previous Record/Request	Enter Preview Mode [...]	Spell Check Found Set
Go to Field [...]	New Record/Request	Toggle Status Area [...]
Go to Next Field	Duplicate Record/Request	Toggle View-as-List [...]
Go to Previous Field	Delete Record/Request [...]	Toggle Window [...]
Sort [...]	Delete Found Set [...]	Home
Unsort	Paste from Index [...]	Page Up
Import Records [...]	Paste Current Date [...]	Page Down
Import Picture...	Paste Current Time [...]	End
Import Movie...	Paste Current User [...]	Send Apple Event [...]
Export Records [...]	Paste Literal [...]	Help...
Page Setup [...]	Replace [...]	Open [...]
Print [...]	Reserialize [...]	Close
Perform Find [...]	Relookup [...]	Save a Copy as [...]
Find All	Undo	Define Fields...
Refind	Cut [...]	Quit
	Copy [...]	

```
Specify External Script

File: "NewAddresses"

Script: [Africa          ▼]

[Change File...]    [Cancel]   [ OK ]
```

EXTERNAL FILE

Click this button to select the external file in an Open-type dialog box.
Once it is selected, the file's scripts are listed in the pop-up menu, as here.

EXTERNAL SCRIPT

When you include the *Perform Script [...]* step in a script, an option lets you specify either a script from the active file or an *External Script*.
Choosing *External Script* displays this dialog box. For example, you might execute a *Copy* step in file A, perform a *Paste* step in file B, and return to file A with an *Open* step.

Apple Events, which let you control an application from within another, are beyond the scope of this book. Before using the dialog box below, study the ready-made scripts included in the *Templates* and *Apple Events Examples* files described in the Appendix.

```
√open application
 open document
 do script

 Other...
```

TARGET
Once you've specified an application, its name replaces "Unknown."

DOCUMENT
The *Open Document* event needs the name of a document as a parameter. The *Specify File...* button lets you select a document.

Specify Apple Event

Target application : " <unknown> "

Send the [do script ▼] event with :

◉ Document   [Specify File...]
○ Field value   [Specify Field...]
○ Script text

┌─ Options ──────────────────────────────────┐
│ ☐ Bring target application to foreground   │
│ ☒ Wait for event completion before continuing │
│   ☐ Copy event result to the clipboard │
└──┘

[Specify Application...]   [Cancel]   [OK]

DO SCRIPT
You can send a script or macro through the *Do Script* Apple Event to applications where scripting is possible, like HyperCard and Excel. You could either write a HyperTalk script inside a field, then send the field value, or check the *Script text* button and write the script inside the box.

FOREGROUND
Depending on the task to be performed, an application can work in the background or should be brought to the foreground.

APPLICATION
Clicking this button lets you choose the application you'll send an Apple Event to.

Specify Event

Specify the event class and type to send:

Event Class [CLAS]   Event ID [DIAL]

[Cancel]   [OK]

OTHER
Choosing *Other...* in the pop-up menu displays this dialog box, where you enter the event's *Class* and *ID*. The event here is the automatic dialing of the HyperCard example (see p. 123).

Appendix

The first part of the Appendix describes the *templates* and *Apple Events examples,* which the Easy Install process puts inside the FileMaker Pro 2.1 folder.

These ready-made files are very useful, and actually several companies publish and sell more templates— mostly inventory, billing, etc. for small businesses. You might customize the design and layout text of a template, but retain its field definitions and scripts.

The second part of the Appendix contains a complete list of the *Functions* that you can use in Calculation fields, followed by a recapitulation of the menus.

You can use templates just as they are, or after copying and adapting them to your needs, by making *Clones* (see p. 57).

You can also copy items that you like—fields, buttons, etc.— and paste them into your files.

Even if you don't ever track contacts or check expenses, you should study the templates simply because they have been created by FileMaker Pro experts and thus represent "state-of-the-art" files. Instead of telling you what the templates do (see the *Templates Guide* about this), these pages point out some of the clever ideas and scripts thought up by these experts.

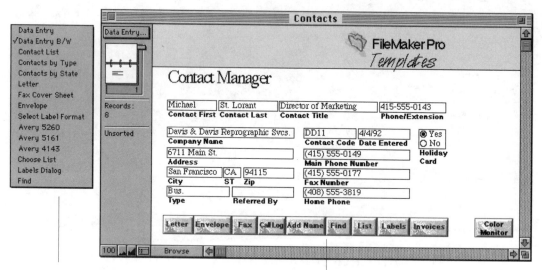

LAYOUTS

Several of the layouts—Letter, Fax Cover Sheet, etc.—retain addresses fields to let you send mail to the person mentioned in the record. Exploring the *Define Fields* dialog box reveals that the *Name* field used for the person's address is a Calculation field containing the formula:
=Contact First&" "&Contact last
This "concatenates" (brings together) the first name and last name of the person and is safer than sliding —e.g., when someone has a very long first name.

BUTTONS

The buttons are made of rectangles and Text objects, with scripts attached to the rectangles.

Letter, Envelope, Fax [Cover Sheet], [Choose] List, and *Labels [Dialog]* simply switch layout. The *Choose List* and *Labels Dialog* layouts show still more buttons, which let you choose a sort order—to list contacts by company or area, etc.—and a label format.

Add Name creates a new record. *Find* displays a simplified request form. *Color Monitor* displays a wider layout—this one is reduced for the 9-inch screen of a Macintosh Classic.

Call Log and *Invoices* copy the Company Name, then call External Scripts. The Lead Tracking or Invoices file is opened, and the Company Name is pasted into a Find request so that the company's calls or invoices can be displayed on screen.

Contacts, Lead Tracking

To explore a template, you might display the *Define Fields* dialog box to see options and formulas, then select scripts in the *Define Scripts* dialog box and click *Edit...* to see the script's steps. There is a faster and better method: print Field Definitions and Scripts (see p. 63). While the information about scripts on screen is somewhat scant, the printed step list is very complete.

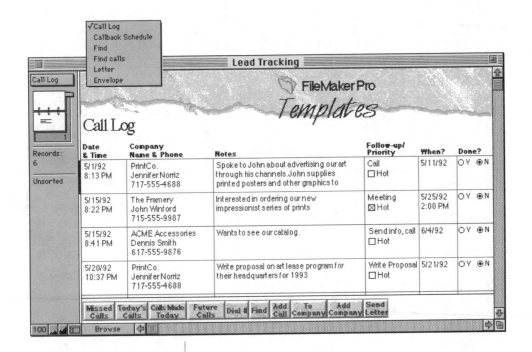

BUTTONS

Missed Calls, Today's Calls and *Calls Made Today* go to the Callback Schedule layout and perform Find scripts. For example, *Missed Calls* finds the records with a past follow-up date (<// in the *Follow-up Date* field) and N checked in the *Done* field.

Future Calls, as well as *Find*, shows a simplified Find request.

Dial # sends two Apple Events to HyperCard. The first one is a HyperTalk dialing script, which resides in a hidden Calculation field with the formula: "dial"&""""&Contact Phone&"""". You are in fact sending an expression like *dial "717-555-4688"*. The second one is a script saying, "activate the application that just sent an Apple Event." Note that this way of dialing is different from the *Apple Events Examples* way (see p. 122).

To Company copies the Company name, then performs an external script in the *Contacts* file that pastes the name and finds the company's record. *Add Company* begins in the same manner, but creates a new record in the *Contacts* file.

This is the layout for a color monitor. The Black and White layout is smaller and lacks the picture.

PHOTOGRAPH

Scanned photographs can look very good on a color screen. You can also buy collections of digitized photographs on CD-ROMs, or have your own photographs digitized with the Kodak Photo-CD process.

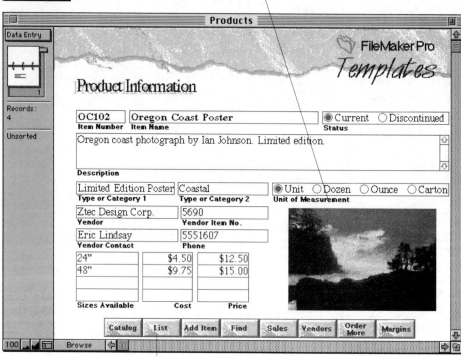

BUTTONS

Most of the buttons let you choose a layout. *Sales* copies the Item Number, then performs an external script to find all the invoices mentioning the item in the *Invoices* file.

The *Margins* button displays the *Margin Report* layout, which has some very simple Calculation fields. Here is a margin formula (returning a percentage) that shows the power of careful field naming: =(Price-Cost)/Cost.

The *Expenses* file lets you keep track of expenses and bills. When you open the file, FileMaker Pro performs a *Startup Script* that does two things:

1) Finds records with data in the Expenses or Deposit field—excluding unpaid bills. 2) Sorts these records by date.

You can define a script as a Startup Script in *Document Preferences* (see p. 59).

BUTTONS

The *Reports* button takes you to the Reports layout, where several buttons let you perform scripts leading to the other layouts. For example, a *Monthly Expense Report sorted by Category 1* button goes to layout Expense Report 1, sorts the file by month and by category 1, then switches to Preview mode so that Sub-Summary fields for expenses by category and month become visible.

The *Enter Bills* button displays the Enter Bills layout. This layout has a Calculation field called Balance Due, with the formula:

=If (Expense Amt.>Due,0,Due-Expense Amt.)

Meaning: If you paid more than was due (say gave a tip), 0 appears in the field. Otherwise, *Due-Paid* appears in the field. If you paid exactly what was due, then Due-Paid=0 and 0 also appears in the field.

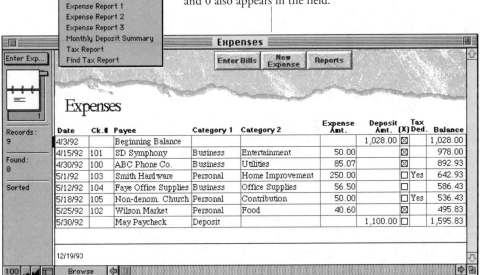

Reports
✓Enter Expenses
Enter Bills
Expense Report 1
Expense Report 2
Expense Report 3
Monthly Deposit Summary
Tax Report
Find Tax Report

	Expenses						

Enter Exp...   Enter Bills   New Expense   Reports

Expenses

	Date	Ck.#	Payee	Category 1	Category 2	Expense Amt.	Deposit Amt.	Tax (X) Ded.	Balance
Records: 9	4/3/92		Beginning Balance				1,028.00	☒	1,028.00
	4/15/92	101	SD Symphony	Business	Entertainment	50.00		☒	978.00
Found: 8	4/30/92	100	ABC Phone Co.	Business	Utilities	85.07		☒	892.93
	5/11/92	103	Smith Hardware	Personal	Home Improvement	250.00		☐ Yes	642.93
Sorted	5/12/92	104	Faye Office Supplies	Business	Office Supplies	56.50		☐	586.43
	5/18/92	105	Non-denom. Church	Personal	Contribution	50.00		☐ Yes	536.43
	5/25/92	102	Wilson Market	Personal	Food	40.60		☒	495.83
	5/30/92		May Paycheck	Deposit			1,100.00	☐	1,595.83

12/19/93

100   Browse

119

APPENDIX TEMPLATES

This invoice template file has many layouts and fields, but the way they work is easy to grasp even if you don't have a Ph.D. in accounting.

The main layout, below, is the user's; the customer receives a version without the *Date Paid*, etc. fields, called simply Invoice.

Note that you don't enter the company's name and address, but only its *Account #*. The program then looks up the rest in the Contacts file. Using one *Customers* or *Addresses* file as the Lookup file for many other files is sensible.

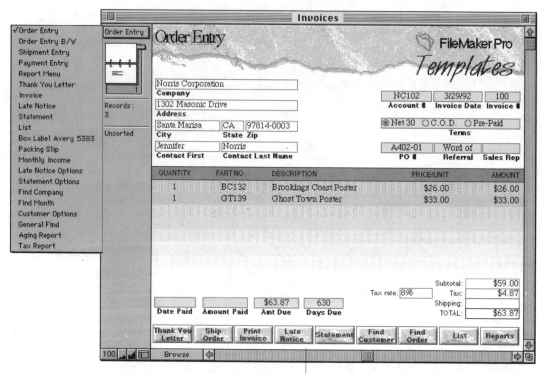

BUTTONS

Most buttons let you choose a layout; some layouts act as menus, with more buttons.

The *Find Customer* button copies the *Account #*, then performs an external script to paste the number in the Contacts file and find it.

The *Aging Report* layout has a Calculation field with the formula:

If (Days Due > 90, "Over 90 days due", If (Days Due > 60, "Over 60 days due", If (Days Due > 30, "Over 30 days due", If (Days Due > 0, "Less than 30 days due","")))) This demonstrates the art of using *If* functions as parameters of *If* functions.

See a complete explanation and another example on p. 127.

If you want to do serious project management with the help of your Macintosh, you may need a more specialized program that lets you handle several tasks simultaneously with color Gantt charts and PERT diagrams, etc.

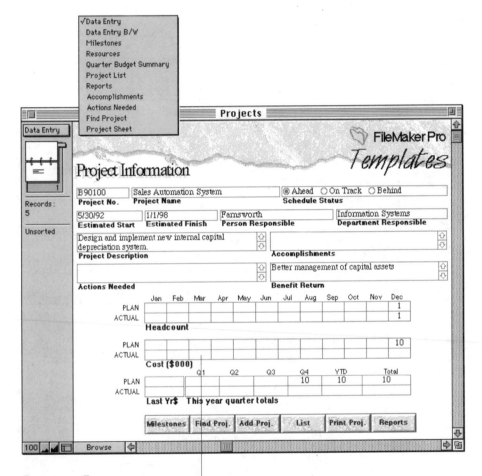

REPEATING FIELDS

The buttons and layouts of this file are similar to those already described in the preceding pages, but this file has at least one interesting feature:

The *Headcount* table is made of two horizontal repeating fields with 12 repetitions each. You might think the *Cost ($000)* table is identical, but in fact it includes two times four horizontal repeating fields with three repetitions each—each field corresponds to one quarter (January+February+March, April+May+June, etc.).

Thus, the *Q1, Q2,* etc. fields in the last table simply add the quarterly repeating fields of the *Cost ($000)* table.

APPENDIX APPLE EVENTS

The *Apple Events Examples* folder contains two FileMaker Pro files: *AE Example-Report Card* (see below) and *FileMaker Events and Objects* (see p. 124), plus some Resolve, Excel and Hyper-Card files.

The Report Card is not very useful as a template (unless you are a schoolteacher), but it contains a very powerful script that links FileMaker Pro to Microsoft Excel or Claris Resolve.

PUPILS

These five records give the test scores of five pupils.
The *Dial* button lets you send a DIAL Apple Event to HyperCard (see p. 113 and opposite page).

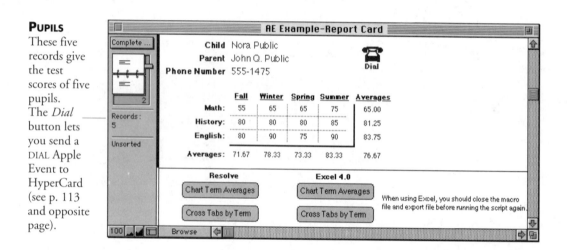

EXCEL CHART

The *Chart Term Averages* button performs a script that exports the scores as a Tab-separated list to a text-only document, then sends three AppleEvents: open the Excel Macro Sheet included in the *Apple Events Examples* folder; open an Excel document called *Export Term*; run the Macro.
The result can be seen at right.
The default Excel chart is ugly, but you can improve it.
The main point is that you can use this button to export data and run any kind of Excel macro; you just have to create the macro with Excel and save it under the name *Excel Bar Chart Script*.

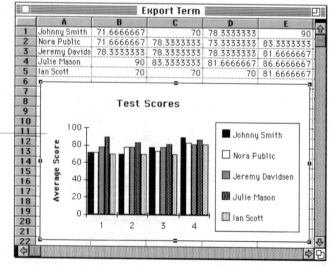

122

AE Example – Report Card

When you click the Phone button, shown on the opposite page, Apple Events are sent to HyperCard. The *Phone Dialing Example* stack (first picture below) lets you choose whether you want to use a phone or a modem.

The *Report Card Browser* is something else altogether. It does not receive Apple Events from FileMaker Pro, but sends them, so that you can pilot FileMaker Pro from within HyperCard. More about this on the next page.

DIALING OPTION

With a modem, you can exchange data—messages and files.

Without a modem, you can dial a regular phone by bringing the handset close to the Mac's loudspeaker.

HyperCard beeps notes that effectively dial the number in the Report Card. Try it!

XCMD

What this stack does is not very interesting: it creates report cards that are nearly identical to those shown on the opposite page.

The interesting part is that it retrieves the data from FileMaker Pro by using "External Commands" (XCMDs) that send the appropriate database Apple Events to FileMaker Pro.

If you know HyperCard and HyperTalk, you can use these powerful XCMDs in your own stacks.

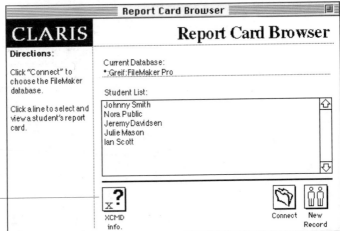

123

APPENDIX APPLE EVENTS

The first picture below shows the opening screen of the *FileMaker Events and Objects* file, which contains records for the 25 Events and 13 Objects supported by FileMaker Pro.

BUTTONS

Introduction to Apple Events explains that Apple Events belong to categories called *Classes* and that related Events and Objects are grouped in *Suites*. *FileMaker Object Map* presents a full list of FileMaker Pro events and Objects grouped according to their Suites (see opposite page). *Objects & Events List* shows the same list in another layout.

FileMaker Events lets you browse the 25 records containing a full description of every Event; *FileMaker Objects* does the same thing for Objects.

FileMaker Object Hierarchy shows the chart below. It tells you that you can define an object as Cell *a* of Row *b* of Table *c* of Database *d* of Document *e* of Application *f*. In FileMaker Pro, Cell=field, Row=record, Table=layout.

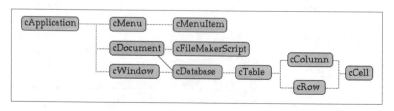

The first picture below shows the *FileMaker Object Map;* the second, a typical Event description.

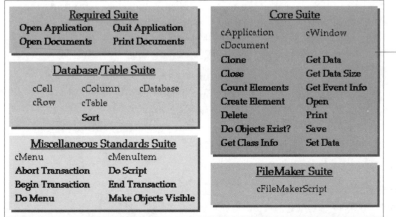

Required Suite

Open Application	**Quit Application**
Open Documents	**Print Documents**

Database/Table Suite

cCell	cColumn	cDatabase
cRow	cTable	
	Sort	

Miscellaneous Standards Suite

cMenu	cMenuItem
Abort Transaction	**Do Script**
Begin Transaction	**End Transaction**
Do Menu	**Make Objects Visible**

Core Suite

cApplication	cWindow
cDocument	
Clone	**Get Data**
Close	**Get Data Size**
Count Elements	**Get Event Info**
Create Element	**Open**
Delete	**Print**
Do Objects Exist?	**Save**
Get Class Info	**Set Data**

FileMaker Suite

cFileMakerScript

SUITES
All applications support the *Required Suite.* The *Core Suite* can also be supported by any application, whereas only spreadsheet and database programs would support the *Database/Table Suite.* Notice that Objects are plain and begin with a "c"; Events are bold.

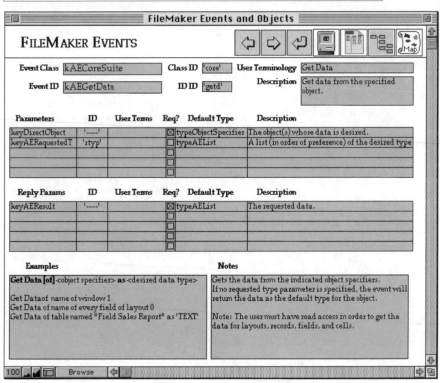

APPENDIX

Functions are used in Calculation field formulas. They "return" a number or a string of characters, which appear in the field as if entered by hand. See examples in the preceding pages.

The name of the function is followed by parentheses, which contain one or several parameters (also called arguments). The kind of parameter(s) that the function needs is given here in italics.

In most cases, parameters are field names or other functions.

For example, **Abs** *(number)* means that you can write Abs (Rate), where "Rate" is the name of a number field.

Sum *(repeating field)* means you can write Sum (Amount), where "Amount" is the name of a repeating field.

Day *(date)* needs the name of a date field as a parameter, or a function like **Today**, but doesn't recognize a string of numbers like 12/18/1994 as a date. As you can use a function as a parameter for another function, the expression Day (TextToDate (12/18/1994)) is legitimate—for a Macintosh with U.S. settings—and returns the number 18.

Here is a full list of FileMaker Pro functions:

Abs *(number)*
Returns the absolute value of *number*.

Atan *(number)*
Returns the arc tangent of *number*.

Average *(repeating field)*
Average of values in non-empty lines of *repeating field*.

Cos *(number)*
Returns the cosine of *number*.

Count *(repeating field)*
Returns the number of valid data entries in *repeating field*. Ignores invalid data, like text in a number field, etc.

Date *(month,day,year)*
Month, *day* and *year* are numbers. Date (12,18,1994) returns the date 12/18/94, formatted according to the date format in the field. Any number is allowed: 15 months are counted as 1 year and 3 months, 32 days in February 1994 as one month and 4 days.

DateToText *(date)*
Returns a string of text equivalent to the 12/18/94 format of *date*, to be used in a text formula or function.
Example: Right (DateToText*(date)*,2) will return the year of *date*, e.g. 94.

Day *(date)*
Returns the day in *date* as a number between 1 and 31.

DayName *(date)*
Returns the name of day in *date*.
Example: DayName (Today) returns Tuesday on 2/8/94.

DayOfYear *(date)*
Returns the number of days from beginning of year until *date*.

Degrees *(number)*
Converts radians to degrees.

Exact *(text1,text2)*
Returns 1 (meaning True) if *text1* and *text2* are identical, 0 (meaning False) if they differ. The comparison is case-sensitive: ABC is different from abc.

Exp *(number)*
Exponential of *number*.

Extend *(non-repeating field)*
Simulates a repeating field with a non-repeating one.
This function could be used in the "Video Sales" example on p. 105. The repeating fields like PriceDin, where the same price must be entered several times, can be replaced by non-repeating fields where the price is entered only once. The formula PriceDin * Din + etc. becomes Extend (PriceDin) * Din + etc.

FV *(payment,interest rate,periods)*
If you pay $100 per month into a 7% savings account for 10 years, the formula FV (100,.07/12,10*12) tells you how rich you'll eventually be.

Hour *(time)*
Returns the "hours" part of a time, i.e. a number between 0 and 12.

If *(test,result1,result2)*
When *test* is true, the function evaluates the expression *result1* and returns it; if *test* is false, the evaluation of *result2* is returned.
Example: If (price>12,"No","Yes") returns

No when the price is too high.
The *test* expression can include the logical operators and/or/not; the *result1* and *result2* expressions can include nested ifs:
If (price>12 and sky=blue,0,if(curr="$",0,1)).
As promised on p. 105, here is a formula that returns the quarter (expressed as a number between 1 and 4) for a date belonging to a field called *Date*:
If (Month *(Date)*<4, 1, If (Month *(Date)*<7, 2,If (Month *(Date)*<10, 3,4)))
In the p. 105 example, the field's name was Month, so instead of Month *(Date)* you would have Month(Month), which may confuse the poor program. It would be safer to change the field's name—but Month can stay as field label.

Int *(number)*
Integer part of *number*. Int (3.9) returns 3.

Last *(repeating field)*
Returns the value of the last non-empty line of *repeating field*. See an example on p. 100.

Left *(text,number)*
Returns the *number* first characters of *text*. Examples:
Left (Country,3) returns the three first letters of the contents of field Country.
Left ("Country",3) returns Cou.

Length *(text)*
Number of characters in text, including spaces.
Several *text* expressions can be "concatenated" with the symbol **&**:
Length (Great&Britain) returns the number of characters in field Great plus the number of characters in field Britain.
Length ("Great"&"Britain") returns 12.

Ln *(number)*
Base-e logarithm of *number*.

Log *(number)*
Base-10 logarithm of *number*.

Lower *(text)*
Converts *text* to lowercase.

Max *(repeating field)*
Returns the highest value in *repeating field*. This can be the greatest number, the latest date or the longest time.

Middle *(text,number1,number2)*
Returns *number2* letters of *text*, starting at letter *number1*.
Example: Middle ("Apple",3,2) returns pl.

Min *(repeating field)*
Lowest value in *repeating field*.

Minute *(time)*
Returns the "minutes" part of *time*, i.e. a number between 0 and 59.

Mod *(number,divisor)*
Returns the remainder of the division of *number* by *divisor*.
Example: Mod (27,5) returns 2.

Month *(date)*
The month in *date* is returned as a number between 1 and 12.

MonthName *(date)*
The month in *date* is returned as a name like January.

NPV *(interest rate, payments)*
This is a variant of the PV function (see opposite page) with unequal payments.
Instead of a fixed *payment* parameter and a *periods* parameter representing the number of payments, the *payments* parameter is here the name of a repeating field which may contain several unequal numbers.

NumToText *(number)*
Returns a string of text similar to the contents of *number*, to be used by a text function.
Example: Length (NumToText (1994)) returns 4.

Pi
This no-parameter function returns 3.1415926535...

PMT *(principal,interest rate,term)*
Returns the payment to be made over the *term* period when *principal* has been borrowed at *interest rate*.
Example: if you borrow $50,000 over ten years at 10% per year, the formula (adjusted on a monthly basis) is
PMT (50000,.10/12,10*12), and returns a monthly payment of $788.40.

Position *(text,string,number)*
Starting at character *number* of *text*, this function scans the text and looks for *string*. If it finds it, it returns the position of its first character; if not, it returns 0.
Example 1:
Position ("the Mac machine","mac",7) returns 9.
Example 2 (from the FileMaker Pro manual):
Left (Name,position(Name," ",1))
finds the first "space" character in field Name, then returns the text from the beginning to this character, i.e. will return "Adam" if the field contains "Adam Morbius."

Proper *(text)*
Converts the first letter of each word in *text* to uppercase and the others to lowercase.
Example: Proper ("APPLE macintosh") returns Apple Macintosh.

PV *(payment,interest rate,periods)*
Returns the present value of *periods* multiplied by *payment* less *interest rate*.

Radians *(number)*
Converts degrees to radians.

Random
This no-parameter function returns a random number between 0 and 1 (but not 0 or 1).
Example: Random*100 returns a random number between 0 and 100.

Replace *(text,number1,number2,string)*
Deletes *number2* characters of *text*, starting at character *number1*, and inserts *string* in their place.
Example: If field Phone contains numbers like 33-0-48-87-28-27 and the phone company replaces 0 with 75, you could create a field NewPhone with the formula
Replace (Phone,4,1,"75").

Right *(text,number)*
Returns the *number* last characters of *text*.
Example 1: Right (Year,2) returns 94 if field Year contains 1994.
Example 2 (from the FileMaker Pro manual):
Right (N,Length (N) - Position (N," ",1)) returns the last name in field N.

Round *(number1,number2)*
Rounds *number1* to *number2* places.

Examples: Round (3.187,2) returns 3.19; Round (3.15,1) returns 3.2; Round (225,-2) returns 200.

Seconds *(time)*
Returns the seconds part of *time*, i.e. a number between 0 and 59.

Sign *(number)*
Returns -1, 0 or 1 according to the sign of *number*.
Example (from the FileMaker Pro manual):
If (Sign(SubscriptEnd - Today) = -1,"Over","").

Sin *(number)*
Sine of angle *number* radians.

Sqrt *(number)*
Square root of *number*.

StDev *(repeating field)*
Returns the standard deviation of entries in *repeating field*.
The pop-up menu in the *Options for summary field* dialog box (see p. 105) offers this function for values in a non-repeating field across several records.

Sum *(repeating field)*
Adds all the values in *repeating field* and returns the total.

Summary *(summary field, break field)*
This function returns the same value as if *summary field* was located in a sub-summary part after a sort by *breakfield*. If *breakfield* is replaced by *summary field* as the second parameter, the whole file is considered (no sort), as in a Grand Summary part.

Tan *(number)*
Tangent of the angle *number* radians.

TextToDate *(text)*

Converts a text date, written in the exact format "12/18/1994" into an official FileMaker Pro date. Use this function or Today to provide a parameter for a date function.

TextToNum *(text)*

Deletes all non-numeric characters from *text*. Example: TextToNum ("2 + 2") returns 22.

TextToTime *(text)*

Converts a text time, written as "09:34:45" into an official FileMaker Pro time, which can be recognized by a time function. Seconds are optional, AM and PM are allowed.

Time *(hours,minutes,seconds)*

Converts three numbers into an official FileMaker Pro time. If there are more than 60 seconds/minutes, the program makes the necessary adjustments. Use TextToTime or Time to provide a parameter for a time function.

TimeToText *(time)*

Converts a time into text, to be used in a text function.

Today

This no-parameter function returns the current date, provided by the Macintosh clock and updated when the file is opened on a new day.

Trim *(text)*

Deletes spaces before and after *text*.

Upper *(text)*

Converts *text* to uppercase.

WeekOfYear *(date)*

Tells you how many weeks have elapsed from the beginning of the year until *date*.

Year *(date)*

Returns the "year" part of *date* (e.g., 1994).

OPERATORS

Mathematical:

/, *, -, +. The usual.

^ Exponent. For example, 5^2 returns 25.

Text:

& Concatenate. If you enter the formula =A&B into field C, then field C will contain the text of field A and the text of field B. See an example on p. 116—and note that the formula is =A&" "&B so that the two texts are separated by a space. If you enter the formula ="A"&"B", the field C will contain the value "AB".

" " Text Constant. Be careful to use "dumb" quotes.

¶ Return Marker. "Blue Planet¶Magazine" equals:

Blue Planet
Magazine.

Comparison (or Boolean):

= Equals. Returns True when both items are equal: 5^2=25 returns True, 1=2 returns False.

≠ or <> Not Equals. Type Option-= for ≠. 1≠2 returns True.

>, < Greater, Less Than. 2<5 returns true.

≥ or >=, ≤ or <= Greater, Less Than or Equal to. Type Option > or < for ≥ or ≤.

Logical:

AND, OR, NOT. These operators are used in If formulas. For example:

If (A>5 AND B≠"Blue Planet",0,1).

Functions listed by category:

CONVERSION

DateToText *(date)*
TextToDate *(text)*
TimeToText *(time)*
TextToTime *(text)*
NumToText *(number)*
TextToNum *(text)*

DATE

Date *(month,day,year)*
Year *(date)*
Month *(date)*
MonthName *(date)*
Day *(date)*
DayName *(date)*
WeekOfYear *(date)*
DayOfYear *(date)*
Today

FIELDS

Average *(repeating field)*
Count *(repeating field)*
Last *(repeating field)*
Max *(repeating field)*
Min *(repeating field)*
Sum *(repeating field)*
StDev *(repeating field)*

Extend *(non-repeating field)*
Summary *(summary field, break field)*

FINANCIAL

FV *(payment,interest rate,periods)*
PV *(payment,interest rate,periods)*
NPV *(interest rate, payments)*
PMT *(principal,interest rate,term)*

LOGICAL

If *(test,result1,result2)*

MATHEMATICAL

Abs *(number)*
Int *(number)*
Ln *(number)*
Log *(number)*
Mod *(number,divisor)*
Pi
Random
Round *(number1,number2)*
Sign *(number)*
Sqrt *(number)*
Exp *(number)*

TEXT

Exact *(text1,text2)*
Left *(text,number)*
Right *(text,number)*
Middle *(text,number1,number2)*
Position *(text,string,number)*
Length *(text)*
Replace *(text,number1,number2,string)*
Lower *(text)*
Proper *(text)*
Upper *(text)*
Trim *(text)*

TIME

Hour *(time)*
Minute *(time)*
Seconds *(time)*
Time *(hours,minutes,seconds)*

TRIGONOMETRIC

Atan *(number)*
Cos *(number)*
Sin *(number)*
Tan *(number)*
Degrees *(number)*
Radians *(number)*

File

New...	
Open...	⌘O
Close	⌘W
Preferences...	
Access Privileges	▶
✓Single-User	
Page Setup...	
Print...	⌘P
Import/Export	▶
Save a Copy As...	
Recover...	
Quit	⌘Q

⌦⌘ P
Print without dialog box.

Edit

Undo Typing	⌘Z
Cut	⌘X
Copy	⌘C
Paste	⌘V
Clear	
Select All	⌘A
New Record	⌘N
Duplicate Record	⌘D
Delete Record	⌘E
Delete Found Set	
Paste Special	▶
Replace...	⌘=
Relookup	
Spelling	▶

Select

✓Browse	⌘B
Find	⌘F
Layout	⌘L
Preview	⌘U
Find All	⌘J
Refind	⌘R
Omit	⌘M
Omit Multiple...	⇧⌘M
Find Omitted	
Define Fields...	⇧⌘D
Sort...	⌘S
✓View as List	

Layout

Align to Grid	⌘Y
Ruler Lines	
Rulers	
T-Squares	⌘T
Size	
Sample Data	
Show	▶
Define Parts...	
Layout Options...	
Ruler Settings...	

File: Access Privileges

Define Groups...	
Define Passwords...	
Overview...	

File: Import/Export

Import Records...	
Import Picture...	
Import Movie...	
Export Records...	

Edit: Paste Special

From Index...	⌘I
From Last Record	⌘'
Current Date	⌘-
Current Time	⌘;
Current User Name	⇧⌘N
Date Symbol	
Time Symbol	
User Name Symbol	
Page Number	
Record Number	

Edit: Spelling

Check Selection...	
Check Record...	
Check Found Set...	
Spell Word...	⇧⌘Y
Spelling Options...	
Install Dictionaries...	
User Dictionary...	

Layout: Show

Buttons	
Text Boundaries	
✓Field Boundaries	
Sliding Objects	
Non-Printing Objects	
Non-Printable Area	

Arrange

Group	⌘G
Ungroup	⇧⌘G
Lock	⌘H
Unlock	⇧⌘H
Bring to Front	⇧⌥⌘F
Bring Forward	⇧⌘F
Send to Back	⇧⌥⌘J
Send Backward	⇧⌘J
Align Objects	⌘K
Alignment...	⇧⌘K
Slide Objects...	
Tab Order...	

Format

Font	▶
Size	▶
Style	▶
Align Text	▶
Line Spacing	▶
Text Color	▶
Text Format...	
Number Format...	
Date Format...	
Time Format...	
Picture Format...	
Field Format...	⌥⌘F
Field Borders...	⌥⌘B

Scripts

ScriptMaker™...	
Define Button...	
Africa	⌘1
Asia	⌘2
Europe	⌘3
Latin America	⌘4

Window

Hide Window	
✓ClubLetter	
Contents	
(Clubs)	

Format: Size

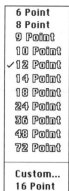

⇧⌘< Next size on menu

⇧⌘> Previous size

⌥⇧⌘< Size up 1 pt

⌥⇧⌘> Size down 1 pt

6 Point
8 Point
9 Point
10 Point
✓12 Point
14 Point
18 Point
24 Point
36 Point
48 Point
72 Point
Custom...
16 Point

Format: Style

✓Plain Text	⇧⌘P
Bold	⇧⌘B
Italic	⇧⌘I
Outline	⇧⌘O
Shadow	⇧⌘S
Underline	⇧⌘U
Word Underline	
Double Underline	
Condense	
Extend	
Strike Thru	
Small Caps	
UPPERCASE	
lowercase	
Title Case	
Superscript	⇧⌘+
Subscript	⇧⌘-

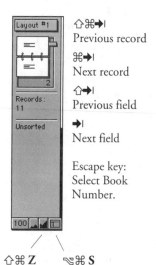

⇧⌘→| Previous record

⌘→| Next record

⇧→| Previous field

→| Next field

Escape key: Select Book Number.

⇧⌘Z   ⌥⌘S

Format: Align Text

✓Left	⌘[
Center	⌘\
Right	⌘]
Full	⇧⌘\

Format: Line Spacing

✓Single
Double
Custom...
2 Point

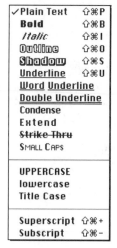

133

INDEX

INDEX

We'd like to hear from you!

Copy and mail or fax this page back to us for more information about other Peachpit books.

I'd like to know more about Peachpit's:

☐ DOS books
☐ Windows books
☐ Books on other topics (specify):

_____

_____

☐ Quantity discounts for (circle):
   Dealers or school trainers
   Corporate/government user groups

Please tell us what you think of this book: _____

_____

_____

_____

_____

_____

Name _____

Organization _____

Address _____

City/State/Zip _____

☐ Check here if you'd rather not receive computer-related information from other companies.

Peachpit Press, Inc.
2414 Sixth Street
Berkeley, CA 94710
Phone: 510/548-4393 ▼ 800/283-9444
Fax: 510/548-5991